Contents

Introduction

This book contains questions designed for the Foundation tier of GCSE Mathematics. It covers the CCEA specification for the modules T1, T2 and T5.

Each chapter matches one in the CCEA Foundation GCSE textbook. This book can be used in conjunction with the textbook or separately on its own. Some of the larger chapters have more than one exercise.

On the contents page, the chapters indicated by an arrowhead are T5.

There are lots of questions in each chapter to provide practice, build confidence and produce satisfaction in being able to do Mathematics. There are problem-solving questions that give opportunities for Mathematics to be used in every day contexts. The questions usually start out by being quite straightforward. Towards the end of each chapter there are some more challenging questions.

Many of the questions can be completed without a calculator. When a calculator is used, we encourage every step of the working out to be shown in your solution.

At the start of every chapter there is a brief summary of what you will be covering as you work through the questions.

The book has been designed to help prepare students for the Mathematics GCSE exam. Doing every question in this book will certainly do that!

CHAPTER 1

Types of number 1

This chapter is about

- using the language of number for example odd, even, multiple, factor, prime, square, cube, square root, cube root
- using index notation
- using negative numbers in familiar contexts.

1 Write down only the **odd** numbers from the following list in order of size, smallest to largest.

12, 33, 921, 302, 89, 7, 90, 661

2 Write down only the **even** numbers from the following list in order of size, smallest to largest.

302, 5, 98, 45, 442, 391, 1002, 6

3

Using all four cards, arrange them to make
a the largest possible number
b the smallest possible even number
c the largest possible multiple of 5.

4 List all the factors of

a	35	**b**	20	**c**	13	**d**	28
e	44	**f**	60	**g**	84	**h**	91

5 List the first five multiples of

a	9	**b**	7	**c**	50	**d**	200
e	0.2	**f**	105	**g**	$\frac{1}{2}$	**h**	13

6 List all the prime numbers less than 30.

7 List two prime numbers between 30 and 40.

8 **a** List the common factors of 30 and 45.
  b List the common factors of 9 and 18.
  c List the common factors of 14 and 21.
  d List the common factors of 12 and 20.

9 Express each of these using **index notation**.
  a $3 \times 3 \times 3 \times 3 \times 3$ **b** $4 \times 4 \times 4 \times 4 \times 4 \times 4 \times 4 \times 4$
  c $6 \times 6 \times 6 \times 6$ **d** $11 \times 11 \times 11 \times 11 \times 11 \times 11 \times 11$
  e 5 **f** $2 \times 2 \times 2 \times 2 \times 5 \times 5 \times 5$

10 Use a scientific calculator to evaluate each of these.

   a 16^2 **b** 7^3 **c** 11^4 **d** 16^5

   e 25^5 **f** 4^8 **g** 2^{12} **h** 23^0

11 Evaluate each of these.

   a 6^2 **b** 3^3 **c** $\sqrt{144}$ **d** $\sqrt[3]{125}$

   e 1^6 **f** 15^1 **g** $\sqrt{81}$ **h** 11^2

12 Arrange these numbers in order of size, smallest to largest.

$$2^3,\ \sqrt{9},\ 4^2,\ \sqrt[3]{64}$$

13 Copy and complete each of these.

   a $\square^2 = 64$ **b** $\square^3 = 216$ **c** $\sqrt{\square} = 4$ **d** $\sqrt[3]{\square} = 2$

14

41	12	15	36	1000	125	19	121

   From the list of numbers in the box, write down all the
   a factors of 36   **b** multiples of 5   **c** prime numbers
   d square numbers   **e** cube numbers.

15 Arrange these numbers in order of size, smallest to largest.

   a −34, 15, −47, 9, 56
   b −14, 10, −15, −1, 8

16 Write down the new temperature when

   a 7°C falls by 11°C   **b** −5°C rises by 12°C
   c −7°C falls by 6°C   **d** −17°C rises by 9°C
   e −12°C falls by 17°C   **f** 22°C falls by 47°C
   g −45°C rises by 58°C   **h** 13°C falls by 38°C.

17 David has an overdraft limit of £1000. His current balance is £135. He spends £420 on a new laptop. Calculate his new balance.

18 The maximum daytime temperature in Castlederg one day in January was 3°C. At night the temperature dropped to a minimum of −12°C. By how many degrees Celsius did the temperature fall?

19 On a particular day in February the difference in temperature between Barcelona and Edinburgh is 23°C. The temperature in Barcelona is 19°C. Work out the temperature in Edinburgh.

20 Oisin says 49 is a prime number. Is he right? Explain your answer.

21 Explain why 1 is not a prime number.

22 John says that 1 is a square number and a cube number. Can you think of another number less than 100 which is both a square number and a cube number?

23 Miriam says that all the factors of 8 are also factors of 16. Is she right? Explain your answer.

CHAPTER 2

Working with whole numbers

This chapter is about

- understanding place value
- writing numbers in figures and words
- adding and subtracting whole numbers
- multiplying and dividing whole numbers by 10, 100, 1000
- knowing how to complete long multiplication and division.

Do not use a calculator for any of these questions.

1 Write each number in figures.

    a forty-six thousand, three hundred and ninety-two
    b fifty-two thousand and thirty-five
    c eight million, sixty-five thousand and seventeen

2 Write each number in words.

    a 27 438   **b** 115 901   **c** 13 620 024

3 What is the place value of the digit **3** in each of these?

    a 6324   **b** 8136   **c** 23 504   **d** 573   **e** 30 682   **f** 3 915 464

4 Copy each statement and write down the correct answer from the list of answers given.

    The sum of 18 and 34   612
    The difference between 18 and 34   52
    The product of 18 and 34   16

5 **a** What is the sum of 137 and 56?   **b** What is the sum of 1352 and 989?

6 **a** What is the product of 29 and 47?   **b** What is the product of 123 and 63?

7 **a** What is the difference between 417 and 254?
    b What is the difference between 2730 and 1185?

8 **a** What is 1792 divided by 7?   **b** What is 44 418 divided by 11?

9 Work out each of these.

    a 23×10 **b** 71×100 **c** 123×10 **d** 45×1000
    e 13×100 **f** 377×10 **g** 362×100 **h** $8 \times 6 \times 100$
    i $2 \times 10 \times 3$ **j** $3 \times 100 \times 5$ **k** $6 \times 1000 \times 4$ **l** $4 \times 10 \times 3 \times 10$

10 Work out each of the following.

    a $230 \div 10$ **b** $7100 \div 100$ **c** $730 \div 10$ **d** $45\,000 \div 1000$
    e $130\,000 \div 10\,000$ **f** $3800 \div 100$ **g** $5900 \div 10$ **h** $860\,000 \div 1000$
    i $20\,300 \div 10$ **j** $65\,400 \div 100$ **k** $349\,000 \div 1000$ **l** 8 million $\div 10$

11 Copy the following and fill in the missing numbers.

    a $\square \times 10 = 320$ **b** $\square \div 100 = 86$
    c $\square \div 10 = 12 \times 100$ **d** $\square \times 10 = 5900 \div 10$
    e $\square \times 100 = 32 \times 1000$ **f** $\square \div 100 = 650 \div 10$

12

5	14	27
11	53	37
68	25	2

Select two numbers from the grid which have
a a total of 80 **b** a difference of 20 **c** a product of 28
d a sum of 95 **e** a product of 70 **f** a difference of 31.

13 Pencils come in boxes of 12. How many pencils are there in 25 boxes?

14 In Year 8 there are 3 classes of 28 pupils and 4 classes of 29 pupils. How many pupils are there in Year 8?

15 A farmer sends 924 eggs to a local supermarket. The eggs are packed into boxes of 6. Work out the number of full boxes she sends.

16 Light bulbs come in packs of eight. There are twenty-four packs in a box. A hardware store orders three full boxes. How many light bulbs are there in total?

17 Harry thinks of a number and multiplies it by twenty. The answer is 980. What number did he think of?

18 James' brother is five years older than him. The sum of their ages is 47. How old is James?

19 What number added to 53 000 makes one million?

20 What number subtracted from 2 million gives 684 250?

21 Monica says that when you multiply any number by 10, the answer always ends in zero. Is she correct? Explain your answer.

22 Eugene says that the sum of n and n is the same as the product of a number and n. What is the number?

CHAPTER 3

Lines and angles

This chapter is about

- naming, drawing and measuring straight lines
- knowing what is meant by horizontal, vertical, parallel and perpendicular lines
- naming, drawing, estimating and measuring angles
- knowing the number of degrees in a quarter, half and complete turn
- knowing the eight compass points
- knowing what is meant by acute, right, obtuse, reflex, straight and vertically opposite angles
- calculating missing angles.

1 ABCD is a rectangle.

 a Measure the length of AB in cm.
 b Name the side which is parallel to AB.
 c Name a side which is perpendicular to BC.
 d Name the vertical sides.
 e Name the horizontal sides.
 f Measure the length of diagonal AC in mm.

2 LMNPQ is a pentagon.

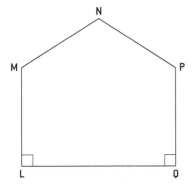

 a Name a vertical line.
 b Name a horizontal line.
 c Name two parallel sides.
 d Name two sides that are perpendicular.
 e Measure the total length of all the sides.

3 Name a quadrilateral that has both parallel and perpendicular sides.

4 Name a quadrilateral that has parallel sides but no perpendicular sides.

5 What name is given to a triangle with perpendicular sides?

6 Copy and complete the table. The first one has been done for you.

	Start facing	Turn	End facing
a	N	$\frac{1}{4}$ turn clockwise	E
b	W	$\frac{3}{4}$ turn anticlockwise	
c	NE	$\frac{1}{2}$ turn	
d	NW	$\frac{1}{4}$ turn anticlockwise	
e		$\frac{1}{4}$ turn clockwise	NE
f		$\frac{3}{4}$ turn clockwise	NE
g	SW	$\frac{1}{8}$ turn anticlockwise	
h	NE	$\frac{1}{8}$ turn clockwise	
i		$\frac{1}{8}$ turn clockwise	W

7 What type of angle is each of the following?

   a 30°   **b** 105°   **c** 90°   **d** 93°   **e** 321°   **f** 360°
   g 142°   **h** 113°   **i** 180°   **j** 5°   **k** 94°   **l** 170°
  m 200°   **n** 340°   **o** 116°   **p** 45°

8 **i** Estimate the size of each of the angles **a**, **b**, **c** and **d**.
    ii Now measure the angles **a**, **b**, **c** and **d**.

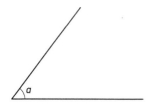

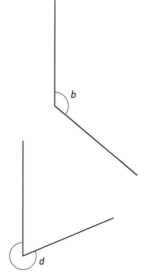

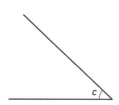

9 Using a protractor or an angle measurer draw and label each of these angles.

   a 75°   **b** 120°   **c** 48°   **d** 162°   **e** 215°   **f** 310°

For questions **10** to **24** work out the size of each angle. The diagrams are not drawn accurately.

10

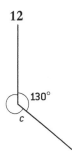

11

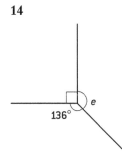

12

13

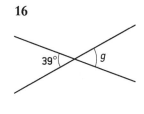

14

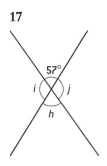

15

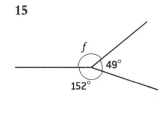

16

17

18

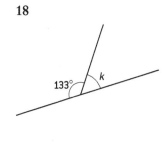

19

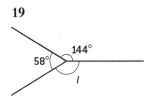

20

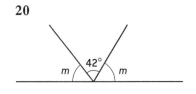

21

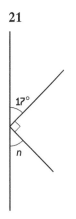

22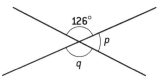

23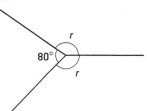

24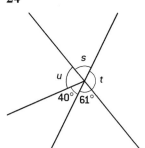

25 Joseph says that the angles 150° and 40° lie on a straight line. Is he correct? Explain your answer.

26 For each statement given, decide if it is **true** or **false**.

  a A full turn can be made up of two reflex angles.
  b A full turn can be made up of four acute angles.
  c A full turn can be made up of one reflex and one obtuse angle.
  d A full turn can be made up of one reflex and one acute angle.
  e A full turn can be made up of two obtuse angles.

CHAPTER 4

Shapes

This chapter is about

- knowing that 2D shapes have two dimensions: length and breadth
- knowing the properties of the different types of triangles
- knowing what a polygon is
- knowing the properties of the different types of quadrilaterals
- knowing the names of the different parts of a circle
- understanding what is meant by congruence
- knowing that 3D shapes have three dimensions: length, breadth and height
- finding the number of edges, faces and vertices for 3D shapes
- drawing and recognising the net of a 3D shape

Exercise A

1   Write down the letter of each of the triangles and match it to its properties.

A – Equilateral triangle

B – Isosceles triangle

C – Right-angled triangle

D – Scalene triangle

1 Two equal sides Two equal angles	**2** All sides equal All angles equal
3 No equal sides	**4** One right angle

2   Write down the letter of each of the quadrilaterals and match it to its properties.

A – Rectangle

B – Kite

C – Square

D – Parallelogram

E – Trapezium

F – Rhombus

1 Two pairs of equal sides One pair of equal and opposite angles	**2** All sides equal Four right angles
3 Two pairs of parallel sides Two pairs of equal sides No right angles	**4** Four right angles Two pairs of equal sides
5 All sides equal No right angles	**6** One pair of parallel sides

3 Name the shapes A to I.

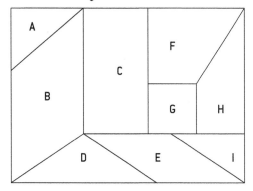

4 Name the shapes X, Y and Z.

5 Write down the names of two shapes that are **not** polygons.

6 Write down the sets of congruent shapes in the grid below.

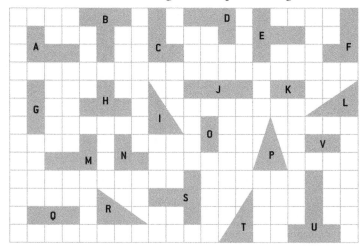

7 a Draw a circle with radius 4 cm.
   b Draw and label a diameter in your circle.
   c Draw and label a chord in your circle.
   d Shade a segment in your circle.

8 a Draw a circle with diameter 6 cm.
   b Draw and label a radius in your circle.
   c Draw and label an arc.
   d Draw and shade a sector in your circle.

9 a Draw a circle with diameter 7 cm.
   b Mark a point X on the circumference of your circle.
   c Draw a tangent to the circle at X.

Exercise B

1 Copy and complete the following table.

Solid	Name	Number of faces	Number of edges	Number of vertices

2 Here is a net for a cube.

	B		
C	F	A	E
	D		

    a When the net is folded to form a cube, write down which face is opposite
       i E   **ii** B.
    b Draw two different nets for a cube.

3 Draw an accurate net for a cuboid with length 4 cm, width 3 cm and height 2 cm.

4 Write down the name of the solid that each of these nets make.

a

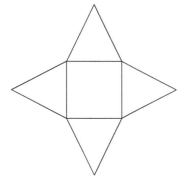

b

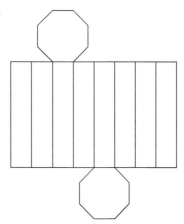

5 Draw an accurate net for each of these solids.

a

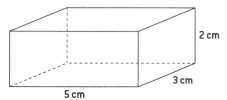

b

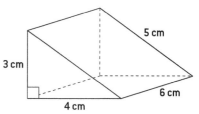

c

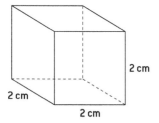

d

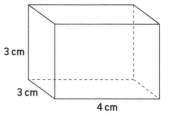

CHAPTER 5

Fractions 1

This chapter is about

- knowing the meaning of a fraction
- being able to find equivalent fractions and simplify fractions
- being able to order fractions
- being able to find a fraction of a quantity

1 What fraction of each shape has been shaded?

a

b

c

d
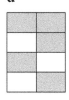

e
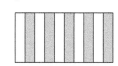

f
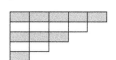

2 Copy the following and fill in the missing numbers for each pair of equivalent fractions.

a $\dfrac{1}{3} = \dfrac{\square}{15}$ **b** $\dfrac{1}{4} = \dfrac{3}{\square}$ **c** $\dfrac{2}{5} = \dfrac{8}{\square}$ **d** $\dfrac{3}{7} = \dfrac{\square}{42}$

e $\dfrac{8}{9} = \dfrac{64}{\square}$ **f** $\dfrac{2}{3} = \dfrac{\square}{36}$ **g** $\dfrac{3}{5} = \dfrac{27}{\square}$ **h** $\dfrac{8}{20} = \dfrac{\square}{220}$

i $\dfrac{3}{4} = \dfrac{\square}{120}$ **j** $\dfrac{11}{12} = \dfrac{77}{\square}$ **k** $\dfrac{8}{12} = \dfrac{\square}{3}$ **l** $\dfrac{35}{40} = \dfrac{\square}{8}$

m $\dfrac{7}{\square} = \dfrac{56}{72}$ **n** $\dfrac{3}{\square} = \dfrac{27}{63}$ **o** $\dfrac{\square}{48} = \dfrac{2}{3}$ **p** $\dfrac{8}{9} = \dfrac{120}{\square}$

3 Write each fraction in its simplest form.

a $\dfrac{4}{8}$ **b** $\dfrac{6}{10}$ **c** $\dfrac{15}{20}$ **d** $\dfrac{12}{18}$

e $\dfrac{14}{16}$ **f** $\dfrac{18}{24}$ **g** $\dfrac{12}{15}$ **h** $\dfrac{20}{25}$

i $\dfrac{45}{60}$ **j** $\dfrac{20}{35}$ **k** $\dfrac{42}{54}$ **l** $\dfrac{28}{35}$

m $\dfrac{18}{27}$ **n** $\dfrac{48}{64}$ **o** $\dfrac{34}{51}$ **p** $\dfrac{70}{91}$

4 Arrange the following fractions in order of size, smallest to largest.

a $\dfrac{3}{8}, \dfrac{1}{4}, \dfrac{1}{3}, \dfrac{1}{6}$ b $\dfrac{3}{10}, \dfrac{2}{5}, \dfrac{1}{2}, \dfrac{7}{20}$ c $\dfrac{13}{20}, \dfrac{5}{12}, \dfrac{3}{5}, \dfrac{7}{15}$ d $\dfrac{5}{8}, \dfrac{7}{16}, \dfrac{9}{20}, \dfrac{3}{5}$

5 Which fraction is the odd one out in each of these?

a $\dfrac{1}{2}, \dfrac{5}{10}, \dfrac{3}{5}, \dfrac{8}{16}$ b $\dfrac{15}{20}, \dfrac{6}{8}, \dfrac{24}{32}, \dfrac{21}{27}$

c $\dfrac{60}{70}, \dfrac{15}{18}, \dfrac{55}{66}, \dfrac{30}{36}$ d $\dfrac{20}{90}, \dfrac{4}{16}, \dfrac{12}{54}, \dfrac{18}{81}$

6 Work out each of these.

a $\dfrac{1}{2}$ of 30 kg   b $\dfrac{1}{4}$ of £52   c $\dfrac{1}{8}$ of 96   d $\dfrac{1}{12}$ of £144

e $\dfrac{1}{10}$ of 34   f $\dfrac{2}{3}$ of £87   g $\dfrac{4}{9}$ of 63 cm   h $\dfrac{3}{8}$ of 72

i $\dfrac{7}{11}$ of £4400   j $\dfrac{3}{10}$ of 72 m   k $\dfrac{7}{12}$ of 360 mm   l $\dfrac{11}{20}$ of £1200

7 In a bag there are 6 red sweets, 8 green sweets and 10 black sweets. What fraction of the sweets is green? Give your answer in its simplest form.

8 In a class there are 12 girls and 15 boys.
   a What fraction of the class are boys?
   b $\dfrac{1}{5}$ of the boys are left handed. How many boys are left handed?

9 Shay spends 3 hours doing homework. During this time he spends 40 minutes doing Maths. What fraction of time is spent on Maths?

10 Clara received £60 for her birthday. She spent a third of it on clothes and a quarter of it on a DVD. What fraction of her money does she have left?

11 School pupils are taking part in an 80 km hike through the Mourne Mountains. On Monday they walk one-fifth of the total. On Tuesday they walk one-quarter of the total. What distance have they covered in the first 2 days?

12 Katie and Finn are reading the same book. Katie says she has read $\dfrac{4}{9}$ of the book and Finn says he has read $\dfrac{6}{13}$ of the book. Who has read the most? Explain your answer.

13 Curtis has 45 periods each week in school. He spends 8 periods each week in Maths, 8 in Chemistry and 9 in Physics. He spends one-quarter of his remaining time doing PE. How many periods of PE does he have each week?

CHAPTER 6

Working with decimals

This chapter is about

- putting decimals in order
- knowing how to add, subtract, multiply and divide decimals
- solving problems involving money
- converting between decimals and fractions
- knowing some common decimal–fraction equivalents.

Do not use a calculator for any of these questions.

1 What is the place value of the digit **5** in each of these numbers?

   a 257   **b** 5401   **c** 12.59   **d** 511   **e** 0.395

   f 56.8   **g** 13.851   **h** 5.36   **i** 52 148   **j** 15 230 120

2 Arrange the following numbers in order of size, smallest to largest.

   a 7.1, 7.13, 7.003, 7.3, 7.06   **b** 1.291, 1.3, 1.25, 1.118, 1.8

3 Work out these.

   a 6.34×10 **b** 9.7×10 **c** 2.183×100 **d** 7.45×100

   e 8.053×1000 **f** 9.6×100 **g** 0.4×10 **h** 0.05×1000

   i 6.1×1000 **j** 0.306×100 **k** 0.0813×1000 **l** 0.0094×10000

4 Work out these.

   a $83.7 \div 10$ **b** $315.9 \div 100$ **c** $6.4 \div 10$ **d** $28.9 \div 100$

   e $647.3 \div 1000$ **f** $8 \div 10$ **g** $13 \div 10$ **h** $0.4 \div 10$

   i $0.617 \div 100$ **j** $5 \div 100$ **k** $2.1 \div 1000$ **l** $24.9 \div 10000$

5 Copy the following and fill in the missing numbers.

   a $2.3 \times \square = 230$ **b** $3.8 \times \square = 38$ **c** $0.77 \times \square = 770$ **d** $15 \times \square = 15000$

   e $850 \div \square = 85$ **f** $107 \div \square = 1.07$ **g** $790 \div \square = 0.79$ **h** $3.6 \div \square = 0.036$

6 Write each decimal number as a fraction in its lowest terms.

   a 0.6   **b** 0.34   **c** 0.45   **d** 0.12   **e** 0.125   **f** 0.08

   g 0.85   **h** 0.405   **i** 0.13   **j** 0.056   **k** 0.004   **l** 0.0003

7 Write each fraction as a decimal number.

   a $\dfrac{1}{10}$ **b** $\dfrac{1}{4}$ **c** $\dfrac{1}{5}$ **d** $\dfrac{7}{10}$ **e** $\dfrac{3}{4}$ **f** $\dfrac{3}{5}$ **g** $\dfrac{3}{20}$

   h $\dfrac{12}{25}$ **i** $\dfrac{11}{100}$ **j** $\dfrac{3}{8}$ **k** $\dfrac{7}{40}$ **l** $\dfrac{7}{1000}$

8 Arrange the following numbers in order of size, smallest to largest.

   a $\dfrac{1}{4}$, 0.23, $\dfrac{1}{5}$, 0.3   **b** $\dfrac{2}{5}$, 0.45, $\dfrac{1}{2}$, 0.403   **c** 0.3, $\dfrac{3}{8}$, 0.32, $\dfrac{39}{100}$

9 Wallace buys three coffees at £1.35 each and two buns costing 65p each. How much change should he receive when he pays with a ten-pound note?

10 A mile is approximately 1.6 km. Approximately how many km is 30 miles?

11 Matthew ran 800 m in 88.34 seconds. Daniel ran 800 m in 93.8 seconds. How much longer did it take Daniel?

12 A roll of ribbon measures 40 m. How many lengths of ribbon each measuring 1.4 m can be cut from the roll?

13 Work out each of the following without a calculator. Show every step.

a 2.3 + 12.74	**b** 8.57 − 2.9	**c** 7 × 0.2	**d** 2.34 ÷ 3
e 1.8 + 25 + 0.39	**f** 24.8 ÷ 5	**g** 5.2 × 6	**h** 4.3 − 1.87
i 2.4 ÷ 0.5	**j** 5.73 × 0.4	**k** 4.02 ÷ 30	**l** 2.59 × 3.11
m 1.789 + 8.6	**n** 6.8 − 2.009	**o** 3.456 × 0.049	**p** 41.76 ÷ 1.2

14 Hilary says that $\frac{5}{8}$ is greater than 0.6 Is she right? Explain your answer.

15 How much bigger is 0.32 than 0.28? Write your answer as a fraction in its lowest terms.

16 Mike earns £88.25 each day he works at the factory. He works every day from Monday to Friday. How much money will he earn in total?

17 Pam shares £23 between her four children so that they each receive the same amount. How much does each child receive?

CHAPTER 7

Percentages 1

This chapter is about

- knowing that 'percentage' means 'number of parts per 100'
- converting percentages to fractions and decimals
- converting fractions and decimals to percentages
- finding percentages of amounts
- recognising recurring decimals
- knowing that recurring decimals are exact fractions, and that some exact fractions are recurring decimals.

1 Express each percentage as a fraction in its lowest terms.

   a 50%   **b** 70%   **c** 45%   **d** 8%   **e** 32%   **f** 17%

   g 6.5%   **h** $33\frac{1}{3}$%   **i** 31.4%   **j** 0.6%   **k** 120%   **l** 0.85%

2 Express each percentage as a decimal.

   a 83%   **b** 14%   **c** 27%   **d** 40%   **e** 9%   **f** 8.5%

   g 12.1% **h** 330%   **i** 0.2%   **j** 140%   **k** 0.05% **l** 3.94%

3 Express each fraction as a percentage.

   a $\dfrac{71}{100}$ **b** $\dfrac{1}{5}$ **c** $\dfrac{9}{10}$ **d** $\dfrac{3}{4}$ **e** $\dfrac{3}{100}$ **f** $\dfrac{11}{20}$

   g $\dfrac{13}{25}$ **h** $\dfrac{47}{50}$ **i** $\dfrac{24}{40}$ **j** $\dfrac{39}{60}$ **k** $\dfrac{87}{1000}$ **l** $\dfrac{30}{80}$

4 Express each decimal as a percentage.

   a 0.75   **b** 0.64   **c** 0.12   **d** 0.4   **e** 0.08   **f** 0.036

   g 0.213 **h** 0.7225 **i** 0.0375 **j** 1.2   **k** 1.05   **l** 0.0201

5 Copy and complete the following table.

	Fraction	Decimal	Percentage		Fraction	Decimal	Percentage
a	$\dfrac{3}{10}$			h	$\dfrac{2}{5}$		
b		0.7		i		0.24	
c			60%	j			68%
d		0.36		k		0.85	
e	$\dfrac{1}{8}$			l	$\dfrac{19}{20}$		
f		0.405		m		1.4	
g			2.75%	n			350%

6 Arrange the following values in order of size, smallest to largest.

   a 41%, 0.4, $\frac{44}{100}$ **b** $\frac{3}{5}$, 57%, 0.63   **c** $\frac{3}{4}$, 0.7, 77%   **d** 0.18, $\frac{3}{20}$, 19.5%

7 Sam scored 15 out of 25 in his French test. Express his score as a percentage.

8 Jill scored 17 out of 20 in her Maths exam. Express her result as a percentage.

9 Emma scored 43 out of 50 in her Science test. Express her mark as a percentage.

10 There are 30 pupils in class 8L. Twelve pupils are boys. Calculate the percentage of girls in class 8L.

11 A cake has a mass of 300 g. It contains 75 g of butter. Calculate the percentage of butter in the cake.

12 Without the use of a calculator, find each of these.

   a 10% of £50   **b** 30% of 240 g   **c** 75% of 80 m   **d** 70% of £1200
   e 5% of 350 km   **f** 65% of 200 litres   **g** 90% of £50   **h** 17.5% of £640

13 Using a calculator, find each of these.

   a 34% of 540 m   **b** 71% of £28   **c** 13% of 244 cm   **d** 83% of £246
   e 17% of 860 g   **f** 61% of 568 ml   **g** 53% of 312   **h** 8.5% of £1250

14 Evaluate each of these to the nearest penny.

   a 23% of £12.35   **b** 19% of £3.24   **c** 5% of £1.27   **d** 93% of £67.39
   e 17.5% of £34.20 **f** 2.8% of £12.12   **g** 8.5% of £0.88   **h** 11% of £23.32

15 Write these recurring decimals using dot notation.

   a 0.444 44...   **b** 0.343 434...   **c** 0.143 143 143... **d** 4.373 737...
   e 0.712 121 2...   **f** 5.012 012...   **g** 0.031 931 9...   **h** 3.174 917 49...

16 Write these as decimals without using dot notation.

   a $0.\dot{3}$ **b** $0.\dot{7}$ **c** $0.3\dot{9}$ **d** $0.2\dot{0}\dot{3}$
   e $0.4\dot{2}\dot{1}$ **f** $3.\dot{2}\dot{8}$ **g** $9.1\dot{7}\dot{2}$ **h** $0.\dot{0}93\dot{2}$

17 Write each fraction as a decimal.

   a $\frac{1}{3}$ **b** $\frac{4}{9}$ **c** $\frac{2}{3}$ **d** $\frac{7}{9}$

   e $\frac{5}{6}$ **f** $\frac{1}{12}$ **g** $\frac{4}{15}$ **h** $\frac{4}{7}$

18 Which of the following fractions are recurring decimals?

   $\frac{3}{4}$, $\frac{5}{9}$, $\frac{3}{10}$, $\frac{1}{8}$, $\frac{1}{6}$

19 How much bigger is $\frac{1}{3}$ than $\frac{3}{10}$? Write your answer as a decimal.

20 Ina says $\frac{2}{3}$ is the same as 66%.

   Joy says $\frac{2}{3}$ is bigger than 66%.

   Kay says $\frac{2}{3}$ is smaller than 66%.

   Who is right? Explain your answer.

This chapter is about

■ using skills in arithmetic

Do not use a calculator for any of these questions.

1 Arrange these distances in order of size, smallest to largest.
1.9 km,   2.8 km,   2.12 km,   3.7 km,   2.105 km,   1.87 km

2 Write down the value of the digit that is underlined in each number.
a 34<u>6</u>0	**b** <u>2</u>17	**c** 125<u>8</u>	**d** <u>6</u>2 300
e 12.5<u>6</u>	**f** <u>3</u>8.236	**g** 9815.3<u>8</u>	**h** 9<u>8</u>.037
i 7.38<u>3</u>8	**j** 127.<u>9</u>253	**k** <u>6</u>240.218	**l** 23.123<u>4</u>

3 Work out these.
a 3.8 + 4.3	**b** 8.5 + 7.9	**c** 12.7 + 14.8	**d** 3.34 + 5.27
e 9.7 − 5.3	**f** 6.3 − 2.8	**g** 8.83 − 3.55	**h** 12.34 − 6.79
i 12.45 + 21.54	**j** 7 − 2.44	**k** 3.7 + 4.88	**l** 15.3 − 6.55

4 Work out these.
a 3 × 10	**b** 4 × 1000	**c** 5 × 10 × 100	**d** 3.5 × 10
e 0.75 × 100	**f** 2.38 × 1000	**g** 0.986 × 10 000	**h** 0.05 × 1000
i 234 × 100	**j** 0.040 13 × 10 000	**k** 0.12 × 10 × 100	**l** 8.9 × 100 × 10

5 Work out these.
a 90 ÷ 10	**b** 450 ÷ 100	**c** 8000 ÷ 100	**d** 280 ÷ 100
e 88 ÷ 10	**f** 2350 ÷ 1000	**g** 0.88 ÷ 10	**h** 5.5 ÷ 100
i 37 ÷ 100	**j** 2.8 ÷ 1000	**k** 0.005 ÷ 10	**l** 0.38 ÷ 100

6 Work out these.
a 0.3 × 4	**b** 0.5 × 7	**c** 1.2 × 4	**d** 0.6 × 3
e 2.3 × 7	**f** 4.3 × 8	**g** 3.2 × 12	**h** 1.2 × 21
i 2.7 × 8	**j** 2.38 × 4	**k** 6 × 4.45	**l** 12 × 13.8

7 Work out these.
a 1.8 ÷ 3	**b** 4.8 ÷ 6	**c** 4.77 ÷ 9	**d** 51.8 ÷ 7
e 4.48 ÷ 8	**f** 5.12 ÷ 4	**g** 39.15 ÷ 5	**h** 8.85 ÷ 5
i 12 ÷ 5	**j** 77 ÷ 4	**k** 19.56 ÷ 30	**l** 4.192 ÷ 0.8

8 Find the sum of 235, 83 and 318.

9 Work out the difference between 583 and 229.

10 Find the product of 23 and 58.

11 Share 3450 between 4.

12 On Monday Megan walked 5.8 km. On Tuesday she walked 7.5 km. On Wednesday and Thursday she walked 14.4 km in total. On Friday she walked 1.1 km less than she walked on Monday. How far did she walk in total during her 5-day hike?

13 Mollie buys a box of cereal costing £2.39. She pays for it with a twenty-pound note. How much change should she receive?

CHAPTER 9

Angles in triangles and quadrilaterals

This chapter is about

- knowing that the angles in a triangle add up to 180°
- finding missing angles in triangles
- knowing that the angles in a quadrilateral add up to 360°
- finding missing angles in quadrilaterals.

Exercise A

The diagrams are not drawn to scale.

For questions **1** to **9** find the value of all the lettered angles.

1

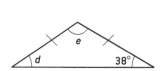

2

3

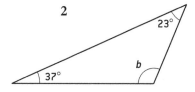

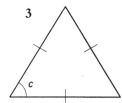

4

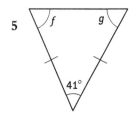

5

6

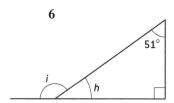

7

8

9

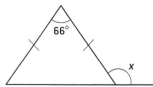

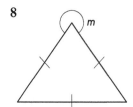

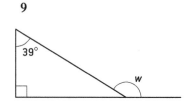

10 Two of the angles in a triangle are 67° and 39°. Find the size of the third angle.

11 Two of the angles in a triangle are 112° and 34°. What type of triangle is it?

12

a

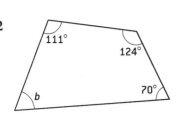

3x

7x

2x

   i Work out the value of *x*.
   ii Work out the size of the three angles.

b

y + 25

2y

2y − 10

   i Work out the value of *y*.
   ii Work out the size of the largest angle.

13 a Construct triangle ABC shown.

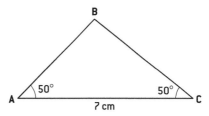

B

50°   50°
A   7 cm   C

  b Measure the length of AB and BC. What do you notice?

14 a Construct triangle DEF.

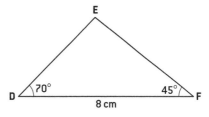

E

70°   45°
D   8 cm   F

  b Measure the length of DE and EF.
  c Measure the angle DEF.

Exercise B

The diagrams are not drawn to scale.

For questions **1** to **3** find the value of all the lettered angles.

1

99°

104°

a

2

111°

124°

b   70°

3

84°

24°

c

37°

4 Three of the angles in a quadrilateral are 102°, 38° and 77°. Find the size of the fourth angle.

5 Two of the angles in a quadrilateral are 88° and 72°. The other two angles are the same size. Work out the size of the other two angles.

6

a

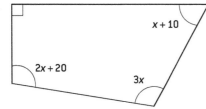

    i Work out the value of x.
    ii Work out the size of the largest angle in the quadrilateral.

b

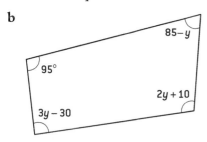

    i Work out the value of y.
    ii Write down the size of the four angles.

7 MNOP is a rectangle.

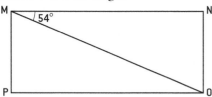

    a What is the size of angle PMO? Give a reason for your answer.
    b What is the size of angle MOP? Give a reason for your answer.

8 ABCD is a parallelogram. Work out the size of

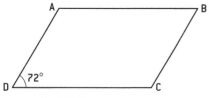

    a angle ABC
    b angle DAB.

9 PQRS is a kite. Work out the size of angle QRS.

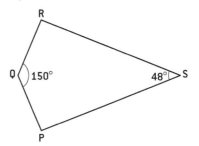

10 For each of the statements given below, say if they are **true** or **false**.
    a A trapezium never has any right angles.
    b A trapezium can have exactly one right angle.
    c A trapezium sometimes has two right angles.
    d A trapezium sometimes has three right angles.

11 EFGH is a rhombus.

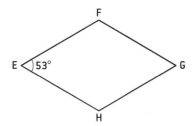

    a Work out the size of angle EFG.
    b The two diagonals intersect at I. Write down the size of angle GIF.

12 Write down the names of three quadrilaterals whose diagonals intersect at right angles.

CHAPTER 10 Parallel lines and polygons

> ## This chapter is about
>
> - knowing what is meant by alternate and corresponding angles
> - knowing what is meant by a regular polygon
> - knowing the names of polygons with five, six, seven, eight, nine and ten sides
> - knowing what is meant by interior and exterior angles of polygons
> - knowing that all the sides are equal in a regular polygon and that all the angles are equal
> - knowing that an interior angle and an exterior angle add up to 180°
> - knowing that the sum of the exterior angles of any polygon is 360°
> - knowing that the sum of the interior angles of an n-sided polygon is $180° \times (n-2)$

Exercise A

1 Study the diagram below. From the list of words fill in the blank spaces below.

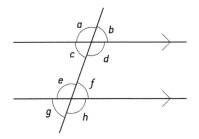

> parallel, alternate
> interior, perpendicular
> adjacent, corresponding
> vertically opposite

  a Angles d and h are _____

  b Angles e and h are _____

  c Angles c and f are _____

  d Angles c and e are _____

2 Look at the diagram below and write down which angle is

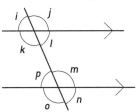

  a vertically opposite j **b** alternate to k

  c vertically opposite n **d** corresponding to j

  e corresponding to k **f** alternate to p.

In questions **3** to **8** find the size of all the lettered angles. Give reasons for your answers.

3

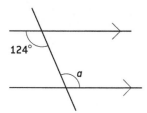

124°

a

4

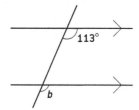

113°

b

5

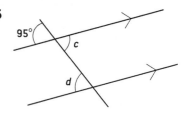

95°

c

d

6

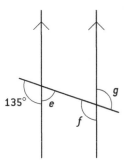

135°

e

f

g

7

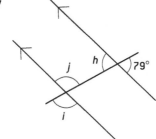

j

h

79°

i

8

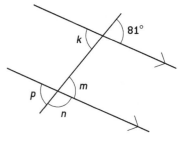

k

81°

m

p

n

9 Find the value of the lettered angles.

a

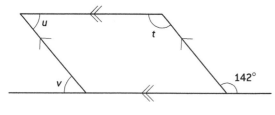

u

t

v

142°

b

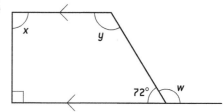

x

y

72°

w

c

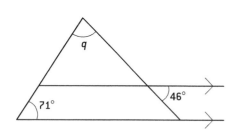

q

71°

46°

d

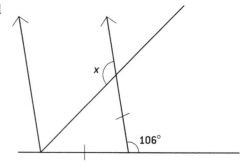

x

106°

Exercise B

Diagrams are not to scale.

1 What name is given to a polygon with:
   a six sides   **b** ten sides   **c** four sides?

2 Find the lettered angles in each polygon.

a

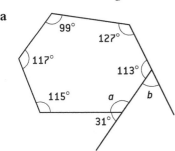

b

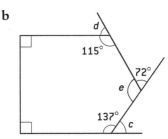

3 For a regular pentagon work out
   a the size of each exterior angle.
   b the size of each interior angle.

4 ABCDEF is a **regular** polygon.

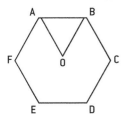

   a Find angle AOB.
   b Find angle FED.
   c Find the sum of the interior angles.
   d Find angle AEF.

5 I am a regular polygon. My exterior angle is 36°. How many sides do I have?

6 I am a regular polygon. My exterior angle is 24°. How many sides do I have?

7 I am a regular polygon. My interior angle is 175°. How many sides do I have?

8 I am a 12-sided regular polygon. Calculate the size of one of my interior angles.

9 I am a 20-sided regular polygon. Calculate the size of one of my exterior angles.

10 Find the sum of the interior angles in a nonagon.

11 Find the sum of the interior angles in a 36-sided polygon.

12 The sum of the interior angles in a polygon is 540°. How many sides does it have?

13 The sum of the interior angles in a polygon is 7380°. How many sides does it have?

14 The interior angles of an octagon are 132°, 140°, 127°, 133°, 114°, 152°, 125° and x. Find the size of angle x.

15 ABCD is a quadrilateral. Explain why the sum of the interior angles is 360°.

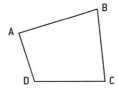

16 Sarah says that she has drawn a regular polygon whose interior angle is 155°. Is she correct? Explain your answer.

CHAPTER 11

Co-ordinates

This chapter is about

- being able to read co-ordinates in all four quadrants
- being able to plot points in all four quadrants.

1   Write down the co-ordinates of each of the points A to I.

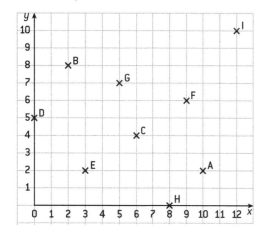

2   Draw a set of axes from 0 to 10 on the x-axis and from 0 to 10 on the y-axis. On the grid plot the following points and label them.

A(3, 5)	B(7, 2)	C(3, 9)	D(4, 0)	E(1, 6)	F(5, 5)
G(0, 3)	H(8, 10)	I(2, 4)	J(10, 10)	K(6, 1)	L(9, 0)

3   Write down the co-ordinates of each of the points O to Z.

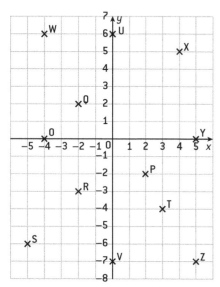

4 Draw a set of axes from −6 to 6 on the *x*-axis and from −6 to 6 on the *y*-axis. On the grid plot the following points and label them.

O(2, 4) P(−3, 1) Q(−3, 4) R(3, −5) S(−4, 0) T(4, −5)

U(−1, −3) V(−4, −2) W(3, −4) X(−1, 5) Y(0, −4) Z(5, −4)

5 Draw a set of axes from −6 to 6 on the *x*-axis and from −6 to 6 on the *y*-axis.
On the grid plot each of the following sets of points.
Join the points with a ruler in the order they appear, joining the last point to the first point in each set.
In each case name the shape formed.

a (3, 3) (3, 5) (5, 5) (5, 3) **b** (−4, 2) (−4, 5) (−2, 6) (−2, 3)
c (3, −1) (3, −4) (5, −4) (5, −2) **d** (−4, −1) (−5, −2) (−4, −4) (−3, −2)
e (3, 1) (6, 3) (6, 1) **f** (2, 1) (2, 5) (0, 3)
g (1, −2) (1, −3) (−2, −3) (−2, −2)

6 Use the grid below to work out each of the messages given here.
a (2, 6) (5, −7) (−1, 7) (−3, −7) (2, −3) (5, −7) (0, 6)
(0, −1) (2, −3) (4, −5) (1, −6) (−3, −7) (−3, 4) (2, −3) (−3, −7)
(−4, −3) (−2, −3) (−5, −6) (−4, −3) (2, −3) (4, −5) (−5, −6) (−3, −7) (−4, −3)

b (−3, −7) (5, −7) (−2, 2) (1, −6) (0, 6) (−4, 0) (4, −5) (−2, 2) (5, 0)
(5, 7) (5, −7) (−3, 4) (5, 7) (2, −3) (−3, −7) (−4, −3) (−3, 4) (2, −3) (−3, −7)
(0, −1) (2, 0) (−2, 2) (2, 6)

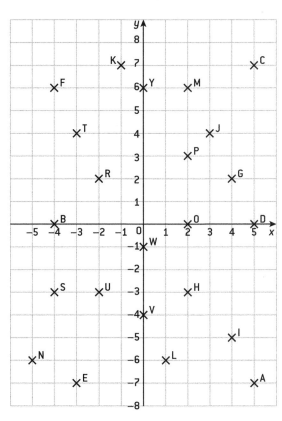

CHAPTER 12 Algebraic expressions 1

This chapter is about

- forming algebraic expressions
- substituting numbers for letters in an algebraic expression to work out its value
- simplifying algebraic expressions by collecting like terms
- multiplying numbers and letters using the rules of algebra.

1 Write down an algebraic expression for each of the following.

   a x plus 10
   b 10 take away y
   c 8 times c
   d d take away 4
   e w divided by 5
   f m times 4
   g 20 divided by e
   h w times w
   i y times x
   j the total mass in kg of two bags weighing 30 kg and x kg each
   k the total cost in pence of five apples costing x pence each
   l the amount of money in £ each child receives when £n is shared between three children
   m the length of timber in metres left after d metres is cut from a 2 m length

2 Conor has x sweets. Write down an expression for the number of sweets each person has.

   a Katie has five more than Conor.
   b Ellie has four less than Conor.
   c Kathy has three times as many as Conor.
   d Mark has two more than Kathy.

3 Alice has n pencils. Write down an expression for the number of pencils each person has.

   a Ronnie has three less than Alice.
   b Leah has four times as many as Alice.
   c Jamie has one less than Leah.
   d Tina has six more than Jamie.

4 Simplify the following expressions.

   a $5x + 3x + x$
   b $8y + 3y - 7y$
   c $2x + 5x - x$
   d $9y - 3y + 5y$
   e $x + x + 4x$
   f $4x + 5x + 8y$
   g $2x + x + 3y + 7y$
   h $9x - 2x + 3y$
   i $5x^2 + 4x^2$
   j $3x + 4y + 2x + 4y$
   k $6x + 5x + 7y - 2y$
   l $3x + 8y - x - 2y$
   m $8x + 7y - 8x - 3y$
   n $9x - 4x - 3y$
   o $4x^2 + 4x + 5x^2 - x$
   p $7x - 10x$
   q $3x + 2y + 12x - 4y$
   r $5y - 4y^2 - 9y + 2y^2 - 3x$

5 Given that $m = 3$, $n = 5$, $p = 12$, $q = 7$, $t = 2$, $x = 10$ evaluate each of the following.

a $n + 4$ **b** $p + q$ **c** $3q$ **d** $p - x$ **e** $m + n - t$

f mx **g** $8nt$ **h** $3p - 9$ **i** $4m + 6$ **j** $2q - 4$

k $xq - n$ **l** $nq + 6m$ **m** $n + 4t$ **n** $3n + 4q$ **o** $10t - 6m$

p $\dfrac{pt}{4}$ **q** $2mn - p$ **r** $3(p - q)$ **s** $mt + qt - 2n$ **t** $(p - q)^2$

u $\dfrac{8x - np}{t}$ **v** $\dfrac{nq}{x}$ **w** $x^2 - q^2$ **x** $\dfrac{mnx}{x - q}$ **y** $(3t)^2$

6 Simplify the following expressions.

a $8 \times p$ **b** $m \times 4$ **c** $5 \times y \times 3$ **d** $t \times 2 \times c$ **e** $w \times w \times 7$

f $3d \times 8d$ **g** $9e \times 7f$ **h** $6g \times 10g$ **i** $6g + 10g$ **j** $h \times h \times h$

k $h + h + h$ **l** $3ef \times 2ef$ **m** $2d \times 11cd$ **n** $3j + 5j - j$ **o** $8x \times 3xy^2$

7 **a** Write down an expression in terms of x for the perimeter of the triangle. Give your answer in its simplest form.

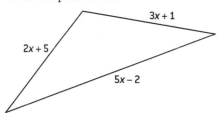

b If $x = 3$ what is the length of the shortest side?

8 Niamh sent n text messages. Oran sent twice as many as Niamh. Pat sent two more than Oran. Write down an expression, in its simplest form, for the total number of text messages sent.

9 A taxi can hold four passengers and a minibus can hold 13 passengers. Write down an expression for the total number of passengers that x taxis and y minibuses can hold.

10

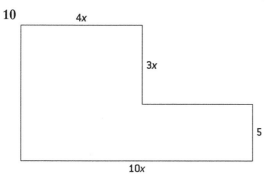

a Write down an expression in terms of x for the shape's perimeter. Give your answer in its simplest form.

b Write down an expression in terms of x for the shape's area. Give your answer in its simplest form.

> **This chapter is about**
>
> - using a decision tree diagram to sort a collection of items
> - obtaining data from a database
> - designing a recording sheet
> - knowing the rules for designing questions in a questionnaire
> - saying why questions are unsuitable
> - suggesting alternative questions
> - designing a questionnaire to test a hypothesis.

Exercise A

1 Use the decision tree diagram to place the following integers. Write down each number with the correct letter A, B, C or D.

6	9	4	8	21	25
35	81	122	169		

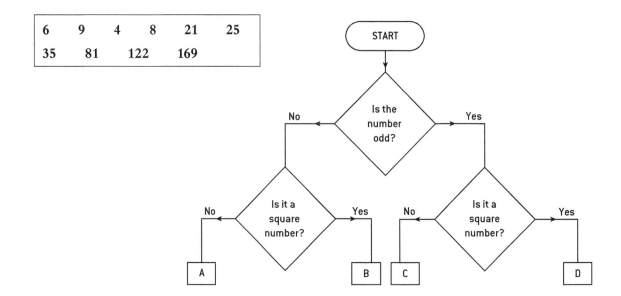

2 Use the decision tree diagram to place the following integers. Write down each number with the correct letter A, B, C or D.

9	7	1	31	2
6	23	33	8	

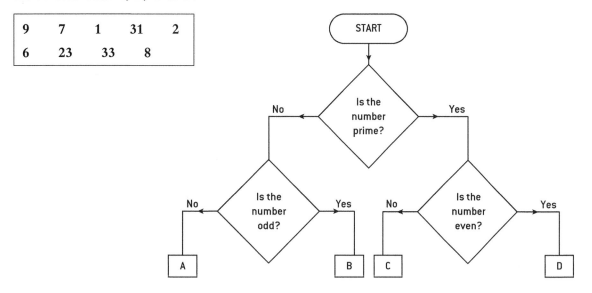

3 Use the decision tree diagram to place the following integers. Write down each number with the correct letter A, B, C or D.

24	2	10	8	5
7	12	1	45	

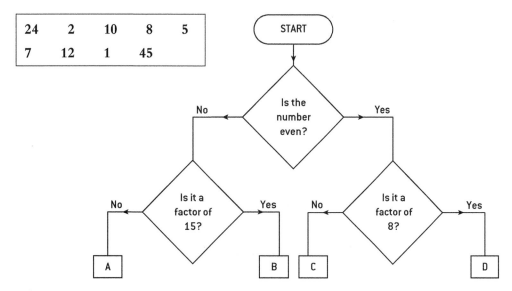

4 Use the decision tree diagram to place the following integers. Write down each number with the correct letter A, B, C or D.

6	8	120	30	45
9	60	15	5	1

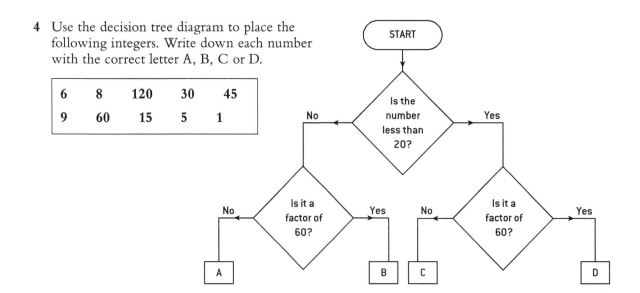

5 The table gives information about the climate in County Tyrone over the past 20 years.

Year	Annual rainfall (mm)	Average temperature (°C)	Highest recorded temperature (°C)	Lowest recorded temperature (°C)
1990	1930	8.3	29	−5
1995	1785	9.2	27	−6
2000	1845	9.1	26	−8
2005	2015	8.7	26	−7
2010	1975	9.5	27	−17

a Which year had the highest annual rainfall?
b Which year had the lowest average temperature?
c Work out the difference between the highest recorded temperature and the lowest recorded temperature in 2010.
d How much more annual rainfall was there in 2005 than in 1995?

6 The table below gives information about four different tractors commonly used by agricultural contractors.

Tractor	Horsepower (hp)	Engine size (litres)	Fuel capacity (gallons)	Mass (kg)
John Deere 6930	155	6.8	66	5878
New Holland 6080	155	6.7	79	6615
Massey Ferguson 6480	145	6.6	70	5818
Fendt 714 Vario	147	6.1	89	6604

a Which tractor has the largest fuel capacity?
b Which tractor produces the least amount of power (hp)?
c Work out the difference in mass between the heaviest and the lightest tractor.
d Francey is a contractor who would like a tractor that is not too heavy but produces a lot of power (hp). Which tractor should he buy? Explain your answer.

Exercise B

1 Kevin is designing a questionnaire and includes this question and response:
How many times do you go to the swimming pool? Please tick appropriate response.

1–3 times ☐   3–5 times ☐   5–7 times ☐   7–10 times ☐

  a Write down one thing wrong with the question.
  b Write down two things wrong with the response section.
  c Rewrite the question and the response section for Kevin.

2 Enda is designing a questionnaire and wants to include this question and response:
Don't you agree that people who play a lot of computer games on the computer end up doing
worse in their exams because they don't have as much time to spend studying?

                                  Yes   No
                                    ☐   ☐

  a Name two things wrong with the question.
  b Name one thing wrong with the response section.
  c Rewrite the question and the response section for Enda.

3 Aoife wants to find out how much people in her home town read. She decides to go to the
library and ask 10 adults how many books they read.
  a Give two reasons why Aoife's results may be biased.
  b Design a question and a response for Aoife's research.
  c Suggest a better method for her research. Include location and sample.

4 Nigel has received a questionnaire through the post about spending on local infrastructure.
One of the questions reads as follows:
Do you not agree that our area needs more money spent on cycle paths?

Strongly agree ☐   Agree ☐   Unsure ☐

  a Name one thing wrong with the question.
  b Name one thing wrong with the response section.
  c Rewrite the question and the response section.

5 Sidney wants to find out what people do at the weekend. He does a survey and includes this
question:
What do you do at the weekend?

Sport ☐   Reading ☐   Shopping ☐   Working ☐   Cleaning ☐

  a Name one thing wrong with the question.
  b Name one thing wrong with the response section.
  c Rewrite the question and the response section for Sidney.
  d Suggest who Sidney should give his survey to.

6 Rewrite each of the following questions to make each one more suitable. Include response sections.
  a Don't you agree that Liverpool is the best football team?
  b How many pizzas do you eat?
  c What television programme will you watch this weekend?
  d Do you agree that eating fruit and vegetables is good for you?

CHAPTER 14

Approximating and estimating 1

This chapter is about

- rounding numbers to the nearest unit, 10, 100 and 1000
- rounding numbers to a given number of decimal places
- rounding numbers to a given number of significant figures
- knowing how to deal with remainders.

1 Write each number correct to the nearest **integer** (whole number).

a	2.3	**b**	5.8	**c**	11.5	**d**	12.1	**e**	34.6	**f**	7.4
g	23.9	**h**	2.79	**i**	3.285	**j**	31.45	**k**	9.49	**l**	19.71
m	341.81	**n**	49.409	**o**	28.078	**p**	207.379	**q**	21.88	**r**	1.23
s	−5.38	**t**	−2.79	**u**	0.221	**v**	−4.29	**w**	−12.15	**x**	−9.499

2 Copy and complete the table below, rounding each number to the nearest 10, 100 and 1000.

	Number	Nearest 10	Nearest 100	Nearest 1000
a	6873			
b	1239			
c	9372			
d	1927			
e	778			
f	12 365			
g	28 771			
h	74 502			
i	365			
j	1111			
k	20 088			
l	19 321			
m	789 267			
n	499 687			
o	999 672			

3 Round each number to **one** decimal place.

a	3.23	**b**	8.75	**c**	31.08	**d**	11.33	**e**	9.49	**f**	6.19
g	21.86	**h**	132.98	**i**	9.501	**j**	2.094	**k**	8.935	**l**	6.049
m	57.97	**n**	3.99	**o**	21.091	**p**	0.46	**q**	3.68	**r**	314.87
s	89.95	**t**	129.949	**u**	1998.957	**v**	47.005	**w**	0.0323	**x**	199.95

4 Round each number to **two** decimal places.

a	9.832	**b**	12.641	**c**	2.037	**d**	98.576	**e**	9.017	**f**	8.949
g	12.902	**h**	1.007	**i**	3.959	**j**	92.783	**k**	9.893	**l**	9.897
m	172.338	**n**	18.9072	**o**	3.227	**p**	78.862	**q**	19.997	**r**	1.895
s	49.997	**t**	0.5992	**u**	1.8481	**v**	0.0031	**w**	2.4971	**x**	1.2367

5 Round each number to **three** decimal places.

a	2.8841	**b**	83.4479	**c**	7.9085	**d**	1.8273	**e**	9.85721	**f**	3.8847
g	0.8147	**h**	1.8035	**i**	9.9898	**j**	12.0042	**k**	1.7733	**l**	34.2928
m	8.7721	**n**	1.2371	**o**	2.3366	**p**	0.8955	**q**	9.1262	**r**	8.0399
s	0.6899	**t**	29.9994	**u**	99.3999	**v**	1.00353	**w**	2.59825	**x**	2.9999

6 Round each number to **one** significant figure.

a	2371	**b**	3865	**c**	53714	**d**	8.4936	**e**	16.283	**f**	0.01432
g	0.007924	**h**	0.01839	**i**	0.9417	**j**	0.9948	**k**	538892	**l**	8046
m	16039	**n**	7.046	**o**	2.0098	**p**	13.019	**q**	7.0034	**r**	0.001403
s	0.06039	**t**	7.9946	**u**	13.964	**v**	26.9999	**w**	0.9963	**x**	0.9999

7 Round each number in question 6 to **two** significant figures.

8 Round each number in question 6 to **three** significant figures.

9 Write each amount of money correctly.

 a £2.084 **b** £89.337 **c** £128.475 **d** £3.5 **e** £0.7 **f** £6.995

10 Use your calculator to work out the following. Write each answer to the given number of decimal places (d.p.) or significant figures (s.f.).

 a $\sqrt{60}$ (1 d.p.) **b** $\sqrt{27}$ (1 d.p.) **c** $\sqrt[3]{22}$ (2 d.p.) **d** $\sqrt[3]{80}$ (2 d.p.) **e** $\sqrt{55}$ (3 d.p.)

 f $\sqrt{600}$ (2 s.f.) **g** $\sqrt[3]{3800}$ (2 s.f.) **h** $\sqrt{23\,634}$ (3 s.f.) **i** $\sqrt{7}$ (3 s.f.) **j** $\sqrt[3]{5}$ (3 s.f.)

11 Aiden rounds 18.946 to one decimal place. Wendy rounds 18.946 to one significant figure. Calculate the difference between their answers.

12 One Saturday in January, 36 800 fans attended a football match in Derby. This number was rounded to the nearest 100. What is the maximum number of fans that could have attended the match?

13 50 children and 10 staff in a nursery school are going to the zoo. Each minibus has 16 passenger seats. How many minibuses are needed?

14 A 4 litre tin of paint covers 75 m². Sammy plans to paint the roof of his shed which has an area of 480 m². How many of these tins of paint does he need to buy?

15 There are four Mars bars in a pack. Yvonne is baking and needs 18 Mars bars. How many packs should she buy?

16 A bag holds 40 kg of sand when full. How many of these bags can be filled from 500 kg of sand?

This chapter is about

■ knowing how to find highest common factor (HCF) and lowest common multiple (LCM) of two numbers
■ writing a number as a product of its prime factors
■ using index notation
■ knowing the index laws for multiplication and division of integer powers.

---

1 List all the factors of 12.

2 List the first five multiples of 12.

3 What is the highest common factor (HCF) of 6 and 8?

4 What is the highest common factor of 18 and 30?

5 What is the lowest common multiple (LCM) of 6 and 8?

6 What is the lowest common multiple of 7 and 10?

7 List all the prime numbers less than 20.

8 Write each number as a product of its prime factors, giving your answer using **index notation**.

a 24	**b** 90	**c** 300
d 147	**e** 825	**f** 420
g 2310	**h** 1800	**i** 612
j 3600	**k** 1750	**l** 888

9 Find the highest common factor of 48 and 112.

10 Find the lowest common multiple of 30 and 120.

11 Find the highest common factor of 144 and 264.

12 Find the lowest common multiple of 18 and 294.

13 For each of the following state whether each statement is **true** or **false**.

a 12 is a factor of 40	**b** 18 is a multiple of 18
c 13 is a factor of 13	**d** 6 is a prime factor of 30
e 1 is a factor of 19	**f** 12 is the HCF of 3 and 4
g 5 is a multiple of 10	**h** 1 is a prime factor of 8

14 In a sweet shop there are 2 large jars of fruit drops. One jar contains 165 orange fruit drops and the other jar contains 210 lemon fruit drops. The owner wants to put fruit drops from each jar into bags for customers to buy. She wants every bag to have the same contents. Every fruit drop must be used.

a What is the largest number of bags she can produce?
b How many of each fruit drop will there be in each bag?

15 Sanco receives a delivery of electronic goods every 15 days. It receives a delivery of stationery every 6 days. Both deliveries came on the 7th August. Work out the next date when both deliveries will be made on the same day.

16 Use a calculator to evaluate each of the following.
    a 14^2 **b** 7^3 **c** 2^5
    d 11^5 **e** 3^4 **f** 6^3
    g 2^8 **h** 11^5 **i** 4^5
    j 25^0 **k** 3.4^3 **l** $(-2)^5$

17 Evaluate each of the following. Show each stage of your working out. Do not use a calculator.
    a $6^2 + 4^2$ **b** $7^2 - 3^3$ **c** 5×2^3 **d** $2^5 \div 4^2$
    e $5^2 \times 2^3$ **f** $5^3 \div 10^2$ **g** $8^2 - 4^3$ **h** $4^2 + 3^2$
    i $9^2 - 8^2$ **j** $2^2 + 3^2 + 4^2$ **k** $\sqrt{10^2 - 6^2}$ **l** $(9 - 4)^2$
    m $2^2(3^3 - 5^2)$ **n** $2^5 - 5^2$ **o** $\sqrt{3^2 + 4^2}$ **p** $\sqrt{2^2 \times 4^2}$

18 Simplify each of the following. Give your answers in **index form**.
    a $2^4 \times 2^5$ **b** 8×8^3 **c** $10^3 \times 10^4$
    d $5^8 \div 5^2$ **e** $9^4 \div 9^3$ **f** $3^{12} \div 3^4$
    g $(6^4)^3$ **h** $(5^7)^2$ **i** $8^5 \div 8$
    j $11^4 \div 11^6$ **k** $4^{10} \div 4^2$ **l** $(4^5)^3$
    m $9^5 \times 9$ **n** $\dfrac{8^2 \times 8^7}{8^3}$ **o** $\dfrac{11^7 \times 11^5}{11}$
    p $\dfrac{5^8 \div 5^2}{5^3}$ **q** $\dfrac{(3^3)^4}{3^3}$ **r** $\dfrac{6^4 \times 6^5}{6^3}$

19 Find the value of n in each of the following.
    a $6^5 \times 6^n = 6^8$ **b** $3^9 \times 3^n = 3^{13}$ **c** $9^n \times 9^7 = 9^{16}$ **d** $4^n \times 4^3 = 4^8$
    e $8^7 \div 8^n = 8^2$ **f** $10^{12} \div 10^n = 10^6$ **g** $7^n \div 7^3 = 7^4$ **h** $2^n \div 2^{10} = 2$

This chapter is about

- being familiar with the units of time
- converting 12-hour clock times to 24-hour clock times
- converting 24-hour clock times to 12-hour clock times
- reading information from timetables.

---

1 Look at the calendar.

   a What date was the second Saturday in April 2011?

   b What date was the first Wednesday in May 2011?

   c What day of the week was 20th March 2011?

APRIL 2011						
Mon	Tue	Wed	Thur	Fri	Sat	Sun
				1	2	3
4	5	6	7	8	9	10
11	12	13	14	15	16	17
18	19	20	21	22	23	24
25	26	27	28	29	30	

2 Convert each of the following times.

   a 3 minutes into seconds   b 2 hours into minutes   c $\frac{1}{2}$ hour into minutes

   d $\frac{1}{4}$ hour into seconds   e 3.5 hours into minutes   f 4.5 minutes into seconds

   g 2 days into hours   h 8 weeks into days   i 1 week into hours

3 Write each of these times using the 12-hour clock format.

   a three o'clock in the afternoon   b eleven o'clock at night
   c half past seven in the morning   d twenty past four in the afternoon
   e ten past one in the afternoon   f five minutes past eight at night
   g twelve o'clock in the afternoon   h quarter to eleven in the morning
   i twenty to six in the morning   j seven minutes past ten at night
   k four minutes past seven in the evening   l quarter to nine in the morning

4 Change each of these times to the 24-hour clock format.

   a 8.00a.m.   b 11.20a.m.   c 3.51a.m.
   d 1.45p.m.   e 6.30p.m.   f 11.59p.m.
   g 10.05a.m.   h 4.47p.m.   i 2.05a.m.
   j 12.18p.m.   k 12.01a.m.   l 11.38p.m.

5 Change each of these times to the 12-hour clock format (use a.m. or p.m.).

   a 1021   b 0610   c 1105
   d 1315   e 2044   f 1225
   g 0311   h 2357   i 0003
   j 1738   k 0941   l 1915

6 A film starts at 8.25p.m. It lasts 85 minutes. What time will it finish?

7 Richard starts milking his cows at 1830. It takes him 2 hours 25 minutes. At what time does he finish?

8 Ruth catches a bus at 1307. The journey time is 78 minutes. At what time does she arrive at her destination?

9 School starts at 9.05a.m. There are nine 35-minute lessons. School finishes at 3.25p.m. How much time altogether do pupils have for break and lunch?

10 Look at the timetable.

Service:	60	60	60
Days of operation:	M-F	M-F	M-F
Calling points:			
Fivemiletown, Bus stop	0745	1415	1700
Murley, Cross	0751	1422	1705
Clabby, Cross	0757	1430	1710
Tempo, Main Street	0805	1440	1720
Garvary, Church	0818	1450	1733
Enniskillen, (Buscentre)	0835	1500	1745

    a **i** What time does the first bus service to Enniskillen leave Fivemiletown bus stop?

         ii How long does the journey to Enniskillen last with this first service?

    b Dominic arrives at Murley Cross at 2.20p.m. and gets on the next bus to Enniskillen. What time will he arrive in Enniskillen?

11 Look at the train timetable from Bangor to Belfast.

Bangor - Belfast   Table 1

Monday - Friday *(all services operate through to Portadown unless stated otherwise)*

Notes	A	B	C	C	C	D	D	D	D		
Bangor	0607	0632	0657	0717	0731	0737	0751	0757	0811	0817	0831	0837	0851	0857	0911	0927	0957
Bangor West	0610	0635	0700	0720	0734	0740	0754	0800	0814	0820	0834	0840	0854	0900	0914	0930	1000
Carnalea	0612	0637	0702	0722		0742		0802		0822		0842		0902		0932	1002
Helen's Bay	0616	0641	0706	0726		0746		0806		0826		0846		0906		0936	1006
Seahill	0619	0644	0709	0729		0749		0809		0829		0849		0909		0939	1009
Cultra	0622	0647	0712	0732		0752		0812		0832		0852		0912		0942	1012
Marino	0624	0649	0714	0734		0754		0814		0834		0854		0914		0944	1014
Holywood	0627	0652	0717	0737	0743	0757	0803	0817	0823	0837	0843	0857	0903	0917	0923	0947	1017
Sydenham ✈	0631	0656	0721	0741		0801		0821		0841		0901		0921		0951	1021
Titanic Quarter	0634	0659	0725	0745	0749	0805	0809	0825	0829	0845	0849	0905	0909	0924	0929	0954	1024
Belfast Central	0638	0703	0728	0748	0753	0808	0813	0828	0833	0848	0853	0908	0913	0928	0933	0958	1028
Belfast Central 🔁	0639	0704	0730	0750	0754	0810	0814	0830	0834	0850	0854	0910	0914	0929	0934	0959	1029
Botanic	0642	0707	0733	0753	0757	0813	0817	0833	0837	0853	0857	0913	0917	0932	0937	1002	1032
City Hospital	0644	0709	0735	0755	0759	0815	0819	0835	0839	0855	0859	0915	0919	0934	0939	1004	1034
Great Victoria Street	0647	0712	0739	0758	0802	0818	0822	0838	0842	0858	0902	0919	0922	0937	0942	1007	1037

    a When does the 0837 train service from Bangor arrive at City Hospital?

    b Anna takes the 0657 train from Bangor to Great Victoria Street. How long does her journey last?

    c Bernadette needs to be at Belfast Central for 8.00a.m. What is the latest train she can catch from Helen's Bay?

    d Carol leaves Bangor on the 0757 train and stops in Holywood for one hour. She takes the next train on to Belfast Central. What time does she arrive at Belfast Central?

    e Danny leaves Holywood on the next train that leaves after 9.30a.m. He needs to be at Belfast Central by 10a.m. The train is delayed by 5 minutes. Will Danny arrive in time?

12 Darragh works from 9a.m. to 5p.m. On a particular day he spent 3 hours and 20 minutes writing a report, a further 1 hour 15 minutes in a conference and a total of 2 hours and 40 minutes on the computer. The rest of the time he spent having his lunch break. How much time, in minutes, did he spend on his lunch break?

> **This chapter is about**
> - knowing the metric units
> - knowing the appropriate metric units to use for common measurements
> - making estimates of length, mass and capacity/volume in metric units
> - knowing how to convert between metric units.

1 Which metric unit of length would you use to measure the following?
  a the length of a pencil
  b the width of a football pitch
  c the distance from Dublin to Cork
  d the height of a windmill
  e the width of a drill bit
  f the circumference of an adult's head

2 Which metric unit of mass would you use to measure the following?
  a the mass of an apple
  b the mass of a digger
  c the mass of a newborn baby
  d the mass of a bag of crisps
  e the mass of an elephant
  f the mass of a paracetamol tablet

3 Which metric unit of capacity would you use to measure the following?
  a the capacity of a can of cola
  b the capacity of a bath
  c the capacity of an electric kettle
  d the capacity of a syringe
  e the capacity of an oil tank
  f the capacity of a baby's bottle

4 Change each of the following measures to the units in brackets.
  a 3 m (cm)
  b 6 km (m)
  c 7 cm (mm)
  d 5000 m (km)
  e 900 cm (m)
  f 40 mm (cm)
  g 8.2 km (m)
  h 35 mm (cm)
  i 120 cm (m)
  j 600 m (km)
  k 2.4 cm (mm)
  l 74 cm (mm)
  m 6.07 km (m)
  n 7 mm (cm)
  o 4.08 m (mm)
  p 2.38 cm (mm)
  q 770 mm (m)
  r 1.9 km (cm)
  s 280 000 cm (km)
  t 7.52 m (mm)

5 Change each of the following measures to the units in brackets.
  a 5 kg (g)
  b 4 tonnes (kg)
  c 7000 mg (g)
  d 4000 g (kg)
  e 2.9 tonnes (kg)
  f 400 g (kg)
  g 4.7 g (mg)
  h 5900 g (kg)
  i 608 kg (tonnes)
  j 3935 mg (g)
  k 570 g (kg)
  l 3.04 kg (g)
  m 13 tonnes (kg)
  n 605 g (kg)
  o 0.3 tonnes (kg)
  p 325 mg (g)
  q 60 g (kg)
  r 0.3 kg (mg)
  s 0.115 tonnes (g)
  t 65 mg (kg)

6 Change each of the following measures to the units in brackets.
  a 6 litres (ml)
  b 2.9 litres (ml)
  c 8000 ml (litres)
  d 4.3 litres (ml)
  e 7200 ml (litres)
  f 10 litres (ml)
  g 1100 ml (litres)
  h 0.3 litres (ml)
  i 1.3 litres (ml)
  j 2.43 litres (ml)
  k 904 ml (litres)
  l 55 ml (litres)
  m 12.8 litres (ml)
  n 321 ml (litres)
  o 15 ml (litres)
  p 80 ml (litres)
  q 7630 ml (litres)
  r 35 litres (ml)
  s 0.0725 litres (ml)
  t 2 ml (litres)

7 A piece of wood is 1.64 m long. Another piece is 75 cm long. What is the total length of the two pieces of wood?

8 How many lengths of tape, each 8 cm long, can be cut from a roll of tape that is 1.2 m long?

9 Arrange these measurements in order of size, starting with the smallest.

    a 3.5 cm, 0.3 m, 45 cm, 82 mm   **b** 1.3 kg, 840 g, 0.75 kg, 1050 g

    c 45 cl, 0.48 litres, 270 ml, 705 ml   **d** 2.4 km, 3360 m, 1.99 km, 2098 m

10 A plank of wood is 8.2 m long. A piece that is 1350 mm long is sawn off one end. What is the length of the remaining plank?

11 The length of one lap of a running track is 400 m. How many times will Martin have to run round the track in order to run a distance of 8 km?

12 How many glasses that each hold 300 ml can be fully filled from a large bottle of cola that contains 2 litres?

13 What is the total weight of the contents of a shopping bag that contains a 1.2 kg bag of potatoes, a large 600 g box of cereal, a small 250 g tub of spread and a multipack containing 12 packets of crisps, with each packet weighing 25 g?

14 Convert each of the following.

    a 6 cm^2 into mm^2 **b** 3.5 cm^2 into mm^2 **c** 5 m^2 into cm^2

    d 2.4 m^2 into cm^2 **e** 800 mm^2 into cm^2 **f** 70 mm^2 into cm^2

    g 60 000 cm^2 into m^2 **h** 47 500 cm^2 into mm^2 **i** 0.3 cm^2 into mm^2

    j 900 000 cm^2 into m^2 **k** 10 000 mm^2 into cm^2 **l** 2.5 km^2 into m^2

15 Convert each of the following.

    a 1 cm^3 into mm^3 **b** 2.7 cm^3 into mm^3 **c** 6 m^3 into cm^3

    d 0.8 m^3 into cm^3 **e** 90 000 mm^3 into cm^3 **f** 1 385 000 cm^3 into m^3

    g 0.04 cm^3 into mm^3 **h** 17.2 m^3 into cm^3 **i** 7 ml into cm^3

    j 30 litres into cm^3 **k** 500 litres into m^3 **l** 3.4 m^3 into litres

16 Arrange these in order of size, starting with the smallest.

    a 1 m^3, $\frac{1}{2}$ litre, 60 ml, 800 cm^3

    b 1 m^2, 120 cm^2, 11 000 mm^2, 0.1 m^2

CHAPTER 18

Statistical averages and spread

This chapter is about

- understanding what is meant by mode, median and mean
- understanding what is meant by the range
- calculating the range, mode, median and mean of a frequency distribution
- finding the limits of the median and modal class of a grouped frequency distribution
- knowing how to use relevant statistical functions on a calculator
- comparing distributions
- choosing the most appropriate statistical average.

1 Find the mean of 12, 18, 15, 11 and 14.

2 Find the mode of 6, 11, 5, 6, 4 and 10.

3 Find the median of 5, 10, 9, 5 and 7.

4 Find the median of 7, 20, 15, 6, 15, 12, 11 and 9.

5 Find the mean length of 64 cm, 29 cm, 50 cm, 62 cm, 34 cm, 58 cm, 52 cm and 61 cm.

6 The test scores in a class were 80%, 70%, 72%, 84%, 90%, 72%, 10%, 72%, 66%, 85%, 92%, 86% and 94%.

   a Find the mean.
   b Find the median.
   c Find the mode.
   d Find the range.

7 The mean of six numbers is 11. The numbers are 12, 7, 15, 10, 10 and x. Find x.

8 The mean of five numbers is 14. Four of the numbers are 10, 18, 17 and 19.

   What is the range of the five numbers?

9 The mean height of 12 girls in a school is 160 cm. The mean height of 8 boys in the same school is 166 cm. What is the mean height of all 20 pupils?

10 In each case write down five numbers which together have:

   a a mode of 8.
   b a median of 10.
   c a mean of 4.
   d a range of 3.

11 Robert rolled the same dice 60 times and recorded his results.

Number on dice	1	2	3	4	5	6
Frequency	12	15	6	3	10	14

Find: a the modal score   b the mean score   c the median score.

12 The scores in a spelling test are recorded in the table.

Score	5	6	7	8	9	10
Frequency	6	4	0	5	7	3

Find: a the mode   b the mean   c the median.

13 Mark has recorded the number of days pupils in his class were absent during the first term.

Number of days	0	1	2	3	4	5	6
Frequency	6	5	8	2	1	6	3

Find: **a** the mode   **b** the mean   **c** the median.

14 Find a single set of three numbers that have a mean of 5, a median of 5 and a range of 4.

15 Find a single set of five numbers that have a mean of 7, a median of 6 and a range of 5.

16 Benn wants to compare the salaries of employees in a large multinational company. He randomly picks five employees and notes their salaries as £23 700, £16 450, £94 400, £32 820 and £27 750.
  a Find the mean.   **b** Find the median.
  c Which average should Benn use to get a representative salary for the staff at the company? Explain your answer.

17 Adam owns a clothes shop. When he is purchasing stock for the autumn and winter collection, which average should he use when deciding on the numbers of each shirt size to order in? Explain your answer.

18 From each table write down:
  i   the modal group   **ii**   the group in which the median lies.
  a

Mass (g)	$0 < m \leq 10$	$10 < m \leq 20$	$20 < m \leq 30$	$30 < m \leq 40$	$40 < m \leq 50$
Frequency	2	6	7	2	8

  b

Volume (cm³)	$30 < V \leq 40$	$40 < V \leq 50$	$50 < V \leq 60$	$60 < V \leq 70$	$70 < V \leq 80$
Frequency	2	4	4	7	5

  c

Children	0–1	2–3	4–5	6–7	8–9
Frequency	9	4	8	3	6

19 In a Science test class 9A had a mean of 77% and a range of 12%. Class 9B had a mean of 82% and a range of 30%.
Using both the mean and the range decide which class has done better in the test. Explain your answer.

CHAPTER 19

Fractions 2

This chapter is about

- converting between improper fractions and mixed numbers
- adding, subtracting, multiplying and dividing fractions

1 Change each improper fraction to a mixed number.

a $\dfrac{7}{5}$ **b** $\dfrac{9}{4}$ **c** $\dfrac{11}{7}$ **d** $\dfrac{13}{2}$ **e** $\dfrac{17}{3}$ **f** $\dfrac{23}{6}$

g $\dfrac{59}{10}$ **h** $\dfrac{27}{8}$ **i** $\dfrac{25}{3}$ **j** $\dfrac{38}{9}$ **k** $\dfrac{48}{11}$ **l** $\dfrac{38}{5}$

m $\dfrac{31}{6}$ **n** $\dfrac{39}{4}$ **o** $\dfrac{60}{7}$

2 Change each mixed number to an improper fraction.

a $3\dfrac{1}{2}$ **b** $2\dfrac{3}{4}$ **c** $4\dfrac{1}{6}$ **d** $1\dfrac{5}{9}$ **e** $2\dfrac{3}{8}$ **f** $2\dfrac{4}{5}$

g $7\dfrac{1}{3}$ **h** $2\dfrac{9}{10}$ **i** $3\dfrac{5}{6}$ **j** $9\dfrac{1}{2}$ **k** $3\dfrac{2}{7}$ **l** $6\dfrac{1}{4}$

m $5\dfrac{3}{8}$ **n** $6\dfrac{5}{6}$ **o** $5\dfrac{4}{9}$

3 Write each decimal number as a mixed number in its lowest terms.

a 5.7   **b** 2.6   **c** 1.4   **d** 12.5   **e** 3.25   **f** 8.09
g 5.13   **h** 6.28   **i** 3.75   **j** 1.44   **k** 6.105   **l** 9.65

4 Write each mixed number as a decimal number.

a $7\dfrac{1}{2}$ **b** $3\dfrac{1}{4}$ **c** $8\dfrac{9}{10}$ **d** $6\dfrac{2}{5}$ **e** $2\dfrac{1}{3}$ **f** $4\dfrac{1}{8}$

g $2\dfrac{3}{20}$ **h** $5\dfrac{7}{100}$ **i** $4\dfrac{7}{11}$ **j** $7\dfrac{13}{20}$ **k** $23\dfrac{3}{4}$ **l** $35\dfrac{1}{6}$

5 Work out the following, giving each answer in its simplest form.

a $\dfrac{2}{7} + \dfrac{3}{7}$ **b** $\dfrac{5}{8} + \dfrac{4}{8}$ **c** $\dfrac{1}{5} + \dfrac{1}{3}$

d $\dfrac{1}{4} + \dfrac{2}{3}$ **e** $\dfrac{3}{10} + \dfrac{2}{7}$ **f** $\dfrac{1}{6} + \dfrac{3}{8}$

g $\dfrac{2}{5} + \dfrac{3}{10}$ **h** $\dfrac{3}{4} + \dfrac{5}{6}$ **i** $\dfrac{4}{7} + \dfrac{3}{5}$

j $\dfrac{7}{10} + \dfrac{5}{6}$ **k** $\dfrac{9}{10} + \dfrac{8}{9}$ **l** $\dfrac{3}{4} + \dfrac{2}{11}$

6 Work out the following, giving each answer in its simplest form.

a $\dfrac{4}{5} - \dfrac{1}{5}$ **b** $\dfrac{7}{8} - \dfrac{1}{3}$ **c** $\dfrac{5}{8} - \dfrac{2}{5}$

d $\dfrac{2}{3} - \dfrac{4}{7}$ **e** $\dfrac{5}{6} - \dfrac{3}{10}$ **f** $\dfrac{7}{12} - \dfrac{1}{5}$

g $\dfrac{3}{4} - \dfrac{1}{6}$ **h** $\dfrac{7}{8} - \dfrac{7}{10}$ **i** $\dfrac{7}{11} - \dfrac{1}{3}$

j $\dfrac{11}{15} - \dfrac{3}{10}$ **k** $\dfrac{17}{20} - \dfrac{5}{8}$ **l** $\dfrac{11}{13} - \dfrac{3}{4}$

7 Work out the following, giving each answer in its simplest form.

a $\dfrac{1}{5} \times \dfrac{1}{3}$ **b** $\dfrac{1}{2} \times \dfrac{5}{6}$ **c** $\dfrac{3}{5} \times \dfrac{1}{7}$

d $\dfrac{3}{5} \times \dfrac{2}{3}$ **e** $\dfrac{3}{4} \times \dfrac{1}{6}$ **f** $\dfrac{5}{8} \times \dfrac{2}{5}$

g $\dfrac{4}{9} \times \dfrac{1}{8}$ **h** $\dfrac{7}{8} \times \dfrac{4}{9}$ **i** $\dfrac{1}{5} \times 60$

j $\dfrac{2}{3} \times 18$ **k** $\dfrac{4}{7} \times \dfrac{3}{4}$ **l** $\dfrac{3}{5} \times \dfrac{5}{3}$

8 Work out the following, giving each answer in its simplest form.

a $\dfrac{1}{5} \div \dfrac{1}{2}$ **b** $\dfrac{1}{8} \div \dfrac{2}{5}$ **c** $\dfrac{1}{3} \div \dfrac{1}{2}$

d $\dfrac{3}{5} \div \dfrac{1}{2}$ **e** $\dfrac{7}{8} \div \dfrac{1}{3}$ **f** $\dfrac{3}{10} \div \dfrac{2}{5}$

g $\dfrac{5}{6} \div \dfrac{2}{3}$ **h** $\dfrac{3}{4} \div \dfrac{5}{8}$ **i** $\dfrac{4}{5} \div \dfrac{4}{5}$

j $\dfrac{1}{3} \div 7$ **k** $8 \div \dfrac{1}{3}$ **l** $\dfrac{2}{3} \div 2$

9 A rectangle has length $\dfrac{3}{7}$ metre and width $\dfrac{1}{4}$ metre. Calculate:

   a the exact area   **b** the exact perimeter.

10 Aaron uses $\dfrac{1}{5}$ of a packet of cereal each day. How many packets of cereal will he need to purchase for his two-week holiday?

11 Roisin uses $\dfrac{3}{5}$ of a pint of milk each day. How many pints will she require for a full week?

12 Robbie, Lydia and Noah share a pizza. Robbie eats $\dfrac{1}{3}$ of the pizza, while Noah eats $\dfrac{2}{5}$ of the pizza. What fraction of the pizza does Lydia eat?

13 Ronan receives money from his great uncle. He puts $\dfrac{1}{4}$ into savings and spends $\dfrac{2}{5}$ on a new TV and sound system. What fraction of the money does he have left?

14 The length of each side of a square is $\dfrac{5}{6}$ cm. Calculate

   a the exact area   **b** the exact perimeter.

CHAPTER 20

Fractions 3

This chapter is about

- adding mixed numbers
- subtracting mixed numbers

1 Work out the following, giving each answer as a mixed number in its lowest terms.

   a $3\frac{1}{2} + 4\frac{1}{2}$ **b** $1\frac{1}{4} + 2\frac{1}{4}$ **c** $2\frac{2}{5} + 3\frac{1}{5}$ **d** $1\frac{1}{3} + 1\frac{1}{2}$

   e $2\frac{2}{5} + 4\frac{1}{3}$ **f** $2\frac{7}{10} + 3\frac{9}{10}$ **g** $5\frac{4}{5} + 4\frac{1}{2}$ **h** $11\frac{7}{10} + 3\frac{2}{3}$

   i $1\frac{5}{6} + 3\frac{2}{3}$ **j** $2\frac{5}{8} + 3\frac{1}{2}$ **k** $1\frac{7}{8} + 2\frac{5}{6}$ **l** $5\frac{3}{4} + 6\frac{4}{5}$

   m $1\frac{2}{7} + 3\frac{4}{5}$ **n** $5\frac{3}{8} + 9\frac{7}{10}$ **o** $1\frac{9}{11} + 2\frac{3}{5}$ **p** $7\frac{5}{12} + 4\frac{5}{6}$

2 Work out the following, giving each answer as a mixed number in its lowest terms.

   a $5\frac{3}{4} - 2\frac{1}{4}$ **b** $4\frac{9}{10} - 1\frac{3}{10}$ **c** $12\frac{5}{7} - 7\frac{2}{7}$ **d** $3\frac{1}{2} - 1\frac{1}{5}$

   e $4\frac{3}{4} - 1\frac{2}{5}$ **f** $3\frac{5}{8} - 1\frac{2}{5}$ **g** $8\frac{8}{9} - 4\frac{3}{4}$ **h** $6\frac{7}{8} - 3\frac{2}{3}$

   i $9\frac{7}{10} - 4\frac{3}{7}$ **j** $10\frac{3}{5} - 4\frac{3}{4}$ **k** $4\frac{2}{5} - 2\frac{5}{6}$ **l** $5\frac{3}{8} - 3\frac{1}{2}$

   m $5\frac{5}{11} - 3\frac{3}{4}$ **n** $5\frac{3}{5} - 4\frac{5}{6}$ **o** $6\frac{4}{5} - 3\frac{7}{8}$ **p** $9\frac{1}{2} - 5\frac{5}{9}$

3 Sonya walked $1\frac{1}{2}$ km on Monday. On Tuesday she walked $2\frac{1}{4}$ km. On Wednesday she walked $2\frac{1}{5}$ km. How far did she walk in total during the three days?

4 Alan ordered $27\frac{1}{2}$ tonnes of fertiliser for his farm. The next day he sowed $3\frac{2}{5}$ tonnes of the fertiliser. How many tonnes are left in the shed?

5 Two friends picked raspberries. At the end of the day they added what they each gathered. Fergal picked $1\frac{3}{5}$ kg and Libby picked $1\frac{1}{15}$ kg more than Fergal.

   a What mass of raspberries did they pick altogether?

   b They need 6 kg of raspberries to make jam. What mass of raspberries do they still need?

CHAPTER 21

Percentages 2

This chapter is about

- calculating percentages of quantities in the context of money
- knowing how to work out percentage profit, loss and discount
- calculating simple interest
- expressing one quantity as a percentage of another.

1 Find:

   a 15% of 300   **b** 35% of 240   **c** 12% of £3200   **d** 9.5% of £274
   e 12.5% of 2400 g   **f** 0.3% of 29 000   **g** 2.5% of £160   **h** 125% of 900

2 Work out these.

   a Increase £30 by 10%   **b** Decrease £80 by 20%   **c** Decrease 120 by 5%
   d Increase £64 by 18%   **e** Increase £250 by 65%   **f** Decrease 30g by 8%
   g Increase 144 kg by 3.5%   **h** Decrease 710 m by 1.6%   **i** Increase £2.21 by 7.1%

3 Aoibhinn buys jeans in a sale. They are marked at £56. There is a discount of 25%. Calculate how much Aoibhinn pays for the jeans.

4 Ann's monthly salary is £2480. She gets a 4% increase in her salary. Calculate the monthly increase in her salary.

5 VAT is added at a rate of 20%. Darren buys a camera priced £1260 without VAT. Calculate the total amount that Darren pays for the camera.

6 In a factory, 2500 light bulbs are produced every hour. It is estimated that 0.2% of these light bulbs will be faulty. How many light bulbs produced every hour will be faulty if the estimate is correct?

7 VAT on electricity is 5%. Hazel receives a bill for £52 without the VAT included. What is the total amount payable for the electricity including the VAT?

8 The population of Anglesville was 38 000 at the end of 2011. During 2012 the population grew by 1.8%. Calculate the population of Anglesville at the end of 2012.

9 **a** Write 6 as a percentage of 25   **b** Write 11 as a percentage of 20
   c Write 27 as a percentage of 36   **d** Write £18 as a percentage of £300
   e Write £2.50 as a percentage of £20   **f** Write 80p as a percentage of £4
   g Express 32 cm as a percentage of 5 m   **h** Express 0.7 as a percentage of 5
   i Express 32 mm as a percentage of 4 cm   **j** Express 2.4 as a percentage of 42

10 Christine attained 68 out of 80 marks in a recent nursing exam. Calculate her percentage.

11 In a class of 30 pupils there are 12 girls. What percentage of the class are boys?

12 There are 11.5 g of sugar in a 21 g bar of chocolate. Calculate the percentage of sugar in the bar.

13 In a Year 10 class, 5 out of the 12 girls travel to school by bus and 9 out of the 13 boys travel to school by bus. Calculate the percentage of pupils in the class that do not travel to school by bus.

14 The number of pupils in a school increases from 800 to 860. What is the percentage increase?

15 In 2010 Arnold had 104 cows on his beef farm. In 2012 he had 118 cows. Calculate the percentage increase in his herd size.

16 Paul bought shares for £6400. He sold them for £6850. Calculate his percentage profit.

17 Janet bought a house in 2007 costing £136 000. She sold it in 2011 for £97 500. Calculate her percentage loss.

18 Find the simple interest when £800 is invested at 4% per annum for 3 years.

19 Find the simple interest when £5000 is invested at 1.5% per annum for 2 years.

20 Maureen invested £1300 at 2.4% per annum simple interest. How much does she have in her account at the end of 5 years?

21 Keith invested £4400 at 1.6% per annum simple interest. How much does he have in his account at the end of 3 years?

22 Find the simple interest when £900 is invested at 3.2% per annum for 6 months.

23 Sean invested £8900 at 2% per annum simple interest. How much does he have in his account at the end of 9 months?

CHAPTER 22 Scale drawings, plans and elevations

This chapter is about

- writing scales in ratio form
- using scales to find actual lengths and lengths on a drawing or map
- making accurate scale drawings
- knowing the meaning of plan and elevation
- drawing plans and elevations.

1 Write each of the following map scales in ratio form.

a 1 cm represents 6 m	**b** 1 cm represents 1.5 m	**c** 1 cm represents 30 m
d 1 cm represents 3 km	**e** 1 cm represents 0.4 km	**f** 1 cm represents 12 km
g 2 cm represents 10 m	**h** 5 cm represents 2 m	**i** 3 cm represents 75 m
j 4 cm represents 1 km	**k** 2 cm represents 0.6 km	**l** 5 cm represents 12 km

2 Given that a map scale is 1 : 10 000 find the actual distance in kilometres for the following measurements on the map.

a 4 cm   **b** 12 cm   **c** 3.5 cm   **d** 23 cm   **e** 21 mm   **f** 5 mm

3 Given that a map scale is 1 : 2 000 000 find the actual distance in kilometres for the following measurements on the map.

a 3 cm   **b** 7 cm   **c** 8.5 cm   **d** 11 cm   **e** 22 mm   **f** 33 mm

4 Copy and complete the following table.

	Scale	Distance on map	Actual distance
a	1 : 10 000	5 cm	
b	1 : 10 000		800 m
c	1 : 200 000	7 cm	
d	1 : 200 000		4 km
e	1 : 1 000 000	2.5 cm	
f	1 : 1 000 000		20 km
g	1 : 50 000	15 cm	
h	1 : 12 500		500 m
i	1 : 15 000	3.4 cm	
j	1 : 2000	14.5 cm	

5 Measure each of the lines accurately.
Using the scale given, work out the actual distance that each line represents.

a _____   1 cm to 5 m

b _____   1 cm to 2 km

c _____ 2 mm to 10 miles

6 a Using a scale of 1 cm = 5 m make a scale drawing of the rectangle.
   b Use your scale drawing to find the actual length of a diagonal of the rectangle.

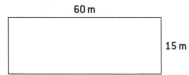

60 m

15 m

7 a Using a scale of 1 cm = 10 m make a scale drawing of the triangle.
   b Use your scale drawing to find the actual length of the third side of the triangle.

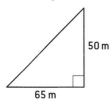

50 m

65 m

8 a Using a scale of 1 cm = 4 m make a scale drawing of the trapezium ABCD.
   b Use your scale drawing to find the actual length of AB and AD.

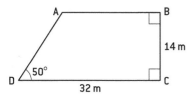

A   B

14 m

50°

D   32 m   C

9 Draw: **i** the side elevation, **ii** the front elevation and **iii** the plan for each solid.

a
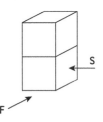
S
F

b
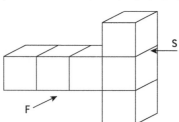
S
F

c
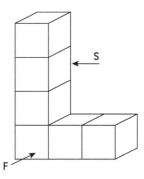
S
F

d
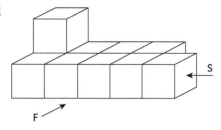
S
F

e
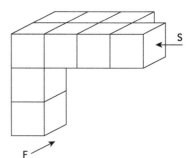
S
F

CHAPTER 23

Statistical diagrams

This chapter is about

- drawing and interpreting pictograms
- drawing and interpreting bar charts
- grouping data
- understanding what is meant by frequency
- distinguishing between continuous and discrete data
- constructing frequency tables
- drawing and interpreting frequency diagrams
- drawing and interpreting stem and leaf diagrams
- drawing and interpreting pie charts.

Exercise A

1   Study the pictogram showing mobile phone sales in a phone shop from Monday to Saturday.

Key: = 4 mobile phones

   a   How many mobile phones were sold on Wednesday?
   b   How many more mobile phones were sold on Saturday than on Friday?
   c   On Thursday five mobile phones were sold. How should this be shown on the pictogram?
   d   How many mobile phones were sold altogether?

2   Draw a pictogram to show the information given about the number of people attending the dentist during one week.
   Monday   10
   Tuesday   9
   Wednesday   3
   Thursday   11
   Friday   5

3 Sophie has drawn a pictogram. Write down three things that are wrong with her diagram.

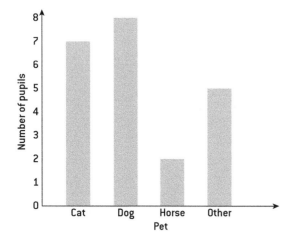

4 Study the frequency diagram showing the favourite pet for pupils in a Year 8 class.

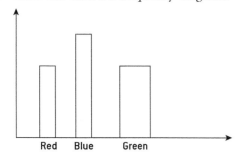

a How many pupils preferred a dog?
b How many more pupils preferred a cat to a horse?
c How many pupils were asked altogether?

5 Draw a frequency diagram to illustrate the number of snacks eaten at break-time.

Toast	50
Pizza	25
Fruit	40
Scones	15

6 Luke has drawn a frequency diagram. Write down three things that are wrong with his diagram.

7 Construct a tally table for the following data which shows the numbers of days pupils in class 8M were absent during the first term at school.

$$
\begin{array}{cccccccccc}
0 & 1 & 2 & 3 & 0 & 2 & 0 & 1 & 2 & 0 \\
1 & 0 & 2 & 1 & 1 & 0 & 1 & 0 & 1 & 4 \\
3 & 1 & 0 & 2 & 5 & 1 & 2 & 4 & 3 & 1
\end{array}
$$

8 Use the groups 0–4, 5–9, 10–14, etc.

    a Construct a grouped tally table for the following data which shows the number of DVDs owned by pupils in class 10A.

$$
\begin{array}{cccccccccccc}
5 & 11 & 3 & 10 & 13 & 4 & 1 & 6 & 4 & 8 & 15 & 3 \\
0 & 3 & 6 & 14 & 11 & 8 & 2 & 13 & 6 & 17 & 12 & 7
\end{array}
$$

    b Draw a grouped frequency diagram to illustrate the data.

9 Use the stem and leaf diagram below to answer the questions that follow.

```
3 | 4 5 8 9              Key:  3 | 8 = 38 marks
4 | 0 2 3 6 8 8
5 | 1 3 3 5 6 7 9
6 | 4 6 8
7 | 0 2
```

    a Find the range.   **b** Find the median.   **c** Find the mean.
    d How many values are less than 46 marks?

10 Ryan has drawn a stem and leaf diagram.

```
5 | 0
6 | 3 8 2 9
8 | 1 6 6
9 | 4 5
```

Write down all the things that are wrong with his diagram.

11 Draw a stem and leaf diagram to illustrate the data given.

$$
\begin{array}{cccccc}
3.5 & 4.1 & 5.6 & 5.1 & 7.2 & 8.6 \\
3.2 & 4 & 7.8 & 6 & 7.9 & 6.5 \\
6.5 & 4.1 & 5.2 & 6.6 & 4.1 & 8.3 \\
6.9 & 4.8 & 3.4 & 3.2 & 3.7 & 5.1
\end{array}
$$

12 The stem and leaf diagram shows the results for boys and girls from 10T in a recent Maths test.

	Boys						Girls				
				5	**0**	1	6				
	9	9	3	3	**1**	2	2	7	8		
8	7	6	4	4	**2**	0	5	6	6	7	
	9	9	6	5	**3**	1	2	4	5		
			2	1	**4**						

Key: 4 | 1 = 41%

From the stem and leaf diagram find:
a the median score for the boys.   **b** the range for the girls.
c the number of pupils in class 10T.   **d** the range for the class.

13 Draw a back-to-back stem and leaf diagram to illustrate the test results for classes 10X and 10Y.

10X
86 86 70 67 68 58 59 91 89
72 67 59 72 99 77 76 94 68
75 77 69 88 88 98 58

10Y
82 74 74 68 65 59 57 73 79
48 50 60 71 58 51 62 53 58
66 64 51 64 73 73

Exercise B

1 Draw and label a pie chart to illustrate the following data which shows the drinks chosen at lunchtime by Year 9 pupils.

Type of drink	Number of drinks	Angle
Water	12	
Orange juice	18	
Milk	10	
Tea	15	
Coffee	5	

2 Draw and label a pie chart to illustrate the following data which shows how pupils in Year 12 travel to school.

How pupils travel to school	Number of pupils
Walk	8
Bicycle	15
Car	21
Bus	40
Train	6

3 Draw and label a pie chart to illustrate the following data which shows pupils' favourite form of exercise.

Form of exercise	Number of pupils
Swimming	6
Running	11
Walking	15
Cycling	8
Other	5

4 Draw and label a pie chart to illustrate the following data which shows the number of animals owned by a farmer.

Type of animal	Cow	Sheep	Horse	Pig	Hen
Frequency	60	35	5	50	30

5 The pie chart shows how 72 pupils in Year 11 travel to school.

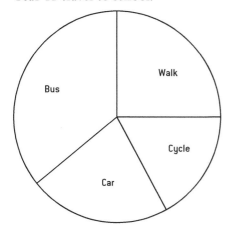

    a What fraction of the pupils in Year 11 cycle to school?

    b How many pupils travel to school by car?

    c How many more pupils walk to school than cycle?

6 The pie chart shows how Kirsty spent her birthday money. She spent £12 on a DVD.

    a What fraction of her money did Kirsty spend buying a DVD?

    b How much money did Kirsty save?

CHAPTER 24

Reading scales

This chapter is about

■ reading scales on a variety of measuring instruments.

For each question, write down the number that each arrow is pointing to.

1
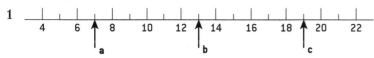

2
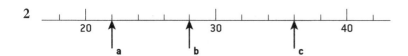

3
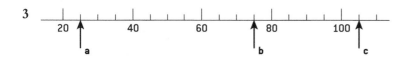

4

5

6
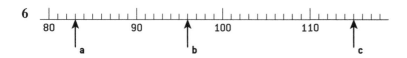

7
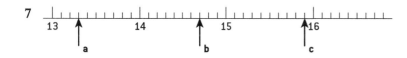

8
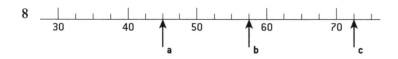

9
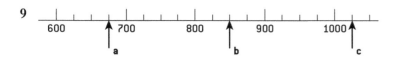

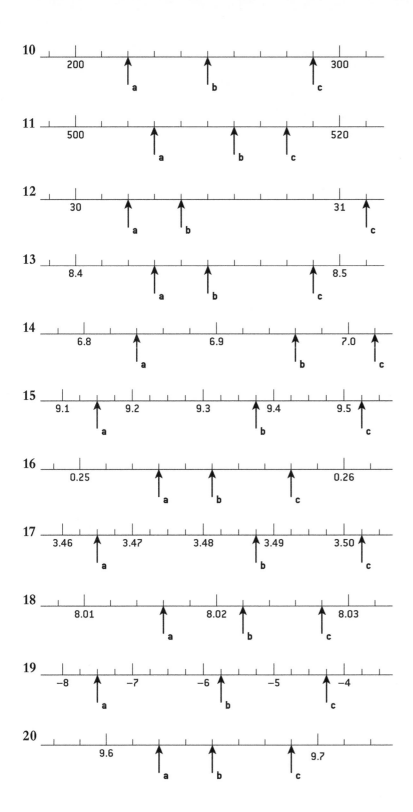

CHAPTER 25 Working with negative numbers

This chapter is about

- knowing how to add, subtract, multiply and divide negative numbers
- knowing that the square root of a positive number can be positive or negative.

1 Work out the following.

a $5 - 7$	**b** $-6 + 2$	**c** $-3 + 3$	**d** $-3 - 3$
e $-7 + 13$	**f** $4 - 12$	**g** $7 - 16$	**h** $-8 - 15$
i $7 + (-2)$	**j** $-7 + (-11)$	**k** $8 - (-3)$	**l** $6 - (+7)$
m $-4 + (-5)$	**n** $-2 - (+10)$	**o** $-5 - (-6)$	**p** $17 - (-9)$
q $-3 + 6 + (-11)$	**r** $-2 - 10 - (-4)$	**s** $6 - 13 - (+5)$	**t** $-9 - (-8) - 4$
u $-13 + (-21) - 11$	**v** $11 - 23 + (-15)$	**w** $-12 - 7 - (-15)$	**x** $-23 - (-44) - 15$

2 Copy and complete the following.

a $\square - 8 = -5$	**b** $\square + 2 = -4$	**c** $5 + \square = -1$
d $4 - \square = 6$	**e** $28 + \square = 0$	**f** $-9 + \square = 3$
g $-2 + \square = 2$	**h** $-17 - \square = -5$	**i** $-9 - \square = 5$
j $\square - 13 = -9$	**k** $\square - (-10) = -3$	**l** $-6 + 3 - \square = -7$

3 Work out the following.

a $3 \times (-4)$	**b** -6×5	**c** -4×7	**d** -9×2
e $-3 \times (-8)$	**f** -2×10	**g** $7 \times (-5)$	**h** -11×5
i $-5 \times (-7)$	**j** $-7 \times (-8)$	**k** $8 \times (-6)$	**l** $(-4)^2$
m $-3 \times 4 \times (-2)$	**n** $-2 \times (-5) \times (-3)$	**o** $(-2)^3$	**p** $(-3)^2 \times (-2)$

4 Work out the following.

a $-20 \div 4$	**b** $30 \div (-5)$	**c** $-18 \div (-3)$	**d** $-42 \div (-6)$
e $32 \div (-1)$	**f** $-24 \div 2$	**g** $28 \div (-7)$	**h** $-40 \div 8$
i $-30 \div (-5)$	**j** $70 \div (-10)$	**k** $-63 \div 9$	**l** $-3 \div 10$
m $(-6)^2 \div (-4)$	**n** $(-4)^3 \div 2$	**o** $-36 \div (-3)^2$	**p** $5^2 \div (-10)$

5 Copy and complete the following.

a $3 \times \square = -15$	**b** $-6 \times \square = 24$	**c** $4 \times \square = -20$
d $-49 \div \square = 7$	**e** $-22 \div \square = 22$	**f** $\square \div 5 = -8$
g $\square \div (-3) = 7$	**h** $\square \div (-10) = 10$	**i** $(-7) \times \square = -56$
j $\square \times -10 = 38$	**k** $-3 \times 2 \times \square = 18$	**l** $-4 \times (-5) \times \square = -10$

6 Write down the two answers to each of the following.

    a $\sqrt{36}$ **b** $\sqrt{100}$ **c** $\sqrt{169}$ **d** $\sqrt{1}$

7 Jacqueline says that when you multiply a number by 10 the answer is always a larger number. Explain why Jacqueline is wrong.

8 Jude says that when you divide a number by 2 the answer is always a smaller number. Is Jude correct? Explain your answer.

CHAPTER 26 Equations 1

This chapter is about

- using letters to represent unknowns
- solving linear equations involving one unknown.

1 Solve each equation.

a $x + 5 = 8$	**b** $x + 10 = 18$	**c** $6 + x = 11$	**d** $x - 3 = 10$
e $x - 4 = 4$	**f** $x - 7 = 12$	**g** $3x = 12$	**h** $5x = 5$
i $4x = 32$	**j** $\dfrac{x}{2} = 6$	**k** $\dfrac{x}{4} = 5$	**l** $\dfrac{x}{3} = 3$
m $x + 7 = 15$	**n** $6x = 24$	**o** $x - 5 = 13$	**p** $\dfrac{x}{5} = 10$
q $3 + x = 17$	**r** $7 - x = 3$	**s** $\dfrac{20}{x} = 5$	**t** $2x = 7$
u $9x = 0$	**v** $3x = 10$	**w** $5x = 11$	**x** $3x = 5$

2 Solve each equation.

a $2x + 3 = 11$	**b** $3x + 1 = 10$	**c** $4x - 2 = 2$	**d** $5x - 7 = 3$
e $2x + 5 = 17$	**f** $3x - 4 = 17$	**g** $8x + 10 = 34$	**h** $4x + 5 = 21$
i $2x - 7 = 7$	**j** $3x + 8 = 8$	**k** $5x - 4 = 31$	**l** $7x - 11 = 17$
m $6x + 4 = 46$	**n** $9x + 11 = 47$	**o** $5x - 8 = 31$	**p** $2x + 5 = 16$
q $3x - 2 = 12$	**r** $4x + 1 = 2$	**s** $5x + 3 = 15$	**t** $2x - 7 = 10$
u $6x - 2 = 3$	**v** $4x + 6 = 20$	**w** $6x - 5 = 10$	**x** $10x - 4 = 4.5$

3 Solve each equation.

a $2x - 3 = -9$	**b** $2x + 3 = 1$	**c** $3x - 1 = -13$	**d** $3x + 8 = 2$
e $5x - 4 = -19$	**f** $2x + 5 = -3$	**g** $2x + 15 = 3$	**h** $6x - 5 = -11$
i $5x + 4 = -11$	**j** $10x - 7 = -47$	**k** $2x + 5 = 1$	**l** $3x - 6 = -33$
m $2x + 9 = 2$	**n** $3x + 5 = 1$	**o** $3x + 1 = -14$	**p** $4x + 3 = 2$
q $5x - 2 = -13$	**r** $5x - 4 = -3$	**s** $4x - 3 = -8$	**t** $5 + 3x = 4$
u $8 + 5x = -3$	**v** $2x - 8 = -9$	**w** $3x - 2 = -4.4$	**x** $3 + 10x = -5$

4 Mya has solved some equations and written down her solution each time.
Check if her solution is correct by substituting her value for x into the equation.
You do not need to solve the equation.

	Equation	Mya's solution
a	$3 + x = 10$	$x = 6$
b	$x - 5 = 12$	$x = 17$
c	$2x + 3 = 11$	$x = 7$
d	$4x - 5 = 5$	$x = 2.5$
e	$7 - x = 3$	$x = 10$

This chapter is about

- drawing or stating the equation of a line parallel to the *x*-axis or *y*-axis
- drawing a straight line given the equation, by calculating co-ordinates and plotting points
- finding the co-ordinates of the point of intersection of two straight lines by drawing the graphs
- knowing that the larger the coefficient of the *x* term in a straight-line equation, the steeper the graph.

1 a Write down the equation of each of the straight lines labelled A to H.
  b Write down the coordinates of the point of intersection of each pair of lines:
  i E and F
  ii G and D
  iii C and D
  iv B and C.

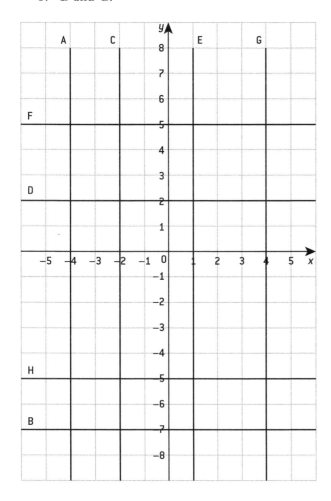

2 Draw a set of axes from −5 to 5 on the x-axis and from −8 to 8 on the y-axis. On your grid, draw and label each of the following lines.

a $x = 4$ **b** $y = 6$ **c** $x = -2$ **d** $y = -5$ **e** $x = 1$
f $y = 8$ **g** $x = -5$ **h** $y = 3$ **i** $x = 0$ **j** $y = -7$

3 Copy and complete the following tables of values for each equation.

a $y = x + 5$

x	0	1	2	3	4
y					

b $y = 4x + 3$

x	0	1	2	3	4
y					

c $y = 5x - 4$

x	0	1	2	3	4
y					

d $y = 3x + 7$

x	0	1	2	3	4
y					

e $y = 2x - 6$

x	0	1	2	3	4
y					

f $y = -2x + 5$

x	0	1	2	3	4
y					

g $y = 12 - 5x$

x	0	1	2	3	4
y					

h $y = -x$

x	0	1	2	3	4
y					

4 For each equation, copy and complete the table of values below from $x = -3$ to $x = 3$.

x	−3	−2	−1	0	1	2	3
y							

a $y = x + 3$ **b** $y = 2x + 4$ **c** $y = 3x - 2$
d $y = 4x + 2$ **e** $y = -3x + 5$ **f** $y = 6 - x$

5 Draw a grid from −6 to 6 on the *x*-axis and −8 to 8 on the *y*-axis.

   a Draw the following four graphs on the same grid. Label each line.

      i $y = 2x + 1$ **ii** $y = x − 2$

      iii $y = −3x$ **iv** $y = 4 − x$

   b Write down the point of intersection of the lines:

      i $y = 2x + 1$ and $y = x − 2$ **ii** $y = x − 2$ and $y = 4 − x$

      iii $y = 4 − x$ and $y = 2x + 1$ **iv** $y = − 3x$ and $y = 4 − x$

6 Write down the gradient of each line.

   a $y = 3x + 2$ **b** $y = 5x − 1$ **c** $y = 6x$ **d** $y = 3 + 4x$

   e $y = 5 + x$ **f** $y = −2x + 7$ **g** $y = 5 − 3x$ **h** $y = 6 − x$

7 Which line is steeper?

   a $y = 2x$ or $y = 8x$ **b** $y = 3x$ or $y = x$

   c $y = 2x + 5$ or $y = 4x − 1$ **d** $y = 2 + 6x$ or $y = 5x + 4$

8 What is the gradient of each line?

a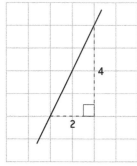

b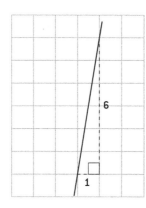

c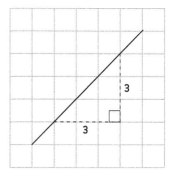

d

e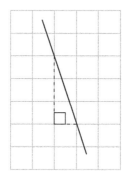

f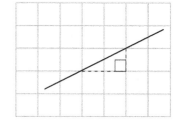

CHAPTER 28

Statistical diagrams 2

This chapter is about

- drawing and interpreting line graphs
- using distance tables
- interpreting two-way tables
- drawing and interpreting scatter graphs
- knowing and recognising the three types of correlation
- using flow diagrams
- drawing and interpreting frequency polygons.

Exercise A

1   The line graph shows the average daily temperature each month in County Antrim over the period of a year.

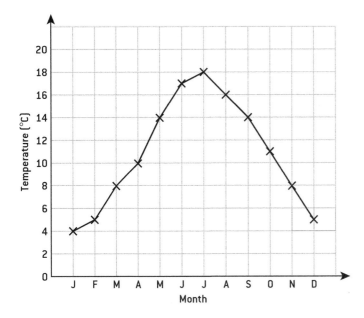

Use the graph to answer the following questions.

   a   What was the average temperature in August?
   b   Between which two months was there the greatest rise in temperature?
   c   In which month was the average temperature the same as the average temperature in March?

2 The following line graph shows the number of customers at a service station at different times during a certain Friday.

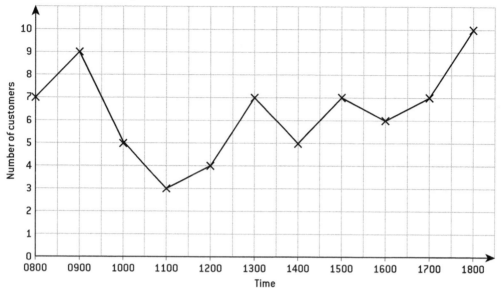

a Use the graph to answer the following questions.
  i At what time was there the largest number of recorded customers at the service station?
  ii Between which two times was there the largest drop in the number of recorded customers at the service station?
b Is it possible to tell how many customers were at the service station at 1030? Explain your answer.

3 The table below shows the age in weeks of a Holstein calf and its mass in kg.

Age (weeks)	1	3	5	7	9
Mass (kg)	44	50	58	69	81

a Draw a line graph to illustrate the information in the table.
b Use your graph to estimate the mass of the calf at 8 weeks.

4 The table below shows the number of pupils absent from school in one week.

Day of the week	Mon	Tues	Wed	Thurs	Fri
Number of pupils absent	10	8	12	17	13

Draw a line graph to show this information.

5 The table below shows the height of a sunflower in cm measured after the given number of days.

Number of days	10	20	30	40	50	60	70	80	90
Height of sunflower (cm)	12	44	59	101	151	183	199	207	209

a Draw a line graph to show the information in the table.
b Use your graph to estimate the height of the sunflower at 45 days.
c When is the sunflower growing at its fastest rate? Explain your answer.

6 The distance table shows the distances in kilometres between different locations in Ireland.

Carlow					
185	Cavan				
192	313	Cork			
218	168	198	Galway		
120	217	85	139	Tipperary	
103	114	259	208	188	Dublin

a Write down the distance between
  i Carlow and Cork   **ii** Galway and Dublin
  iii Cavan and Tipperary   **iv** Cork and Cavan.

b Wesley travelled from Cavan to Cork via Dublin. What was the total length of his journey?

c Owen travelled from Dublin to Galway, stopping in Tipperary on route. Work out how many extra kilometres he covered by not travelling directly from Dublin to Galway.

7 The distance table shows the distances in miles between different locations in Northern Ireland.

Belfast					
36.8	Newry				
68.4	53.6	Omagh			
55.5	79.0	64.0	Coleraine		
40.0	18.2	36.0	60.7	Armagh	
82.3	67.5	26.6	90.8	49.9	Enniskillen

a Write down the distance between
  i Belfast and Newry   **ii** Enniskillen and Omagh
  iii Coleraine and Armagh   **iv** Armagh and Belfast.

b Michael is a delivery driver. He must travel from Belfast to Armagh and then from Armagh on to Omagh. He then returns directly back to Belfast. Work out the total length of his journey.

8 The two-way table shows the number of boys and girls in a class and whether they are left or right handed.

	Left handed	Right handed
Boys	3	11
Girls	4	12

a How many boys are left handed?
b How many girls are right handed?
c How many boys are in the class?
d What fraction of the class is right handed?

9 The two-way table shows favourite TV channels for adults and children.

	BBC 1	BBC 2	ITV	Channel 4
Adults	22	32	17	37
Children	31		33	12

   a Given that 44 in total prefer BBC 2, write down how many children prefer BBC 2.
   b Which is the most popular channel among adults?
   c Which channel do children prefer to watch?
   d Which is the most popular TV channel? Give a reason for your answer.

10 The two-way table gives information on the make of mobile phones owned by men and women.

	iPhone	Nokia	Blackberry	Samsung	TOTAL
Men	5		8	16	
Women		8		11	40
TOTAL	14	19	20		

   a Copy and complete the two-way table filling in all the missing values.
   b How many women owned a Blackberry phone?
   c How many men owned a Nokia phone?
   d How many people were questioned in total?

11 Design a two-way table to record the type of pets that boys and girls in a Year 8 class own.

Exercise B

1 For each scatter diagram describe the type of correlation.

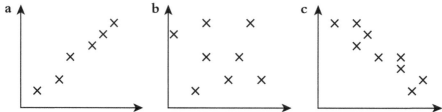

2 State whether you would expect positive correlation, negative correlation or no correlation between the data given in the following.
   a The snowfall in a month and the heating costs for homes that month.
   b The distances travelled by 30 lorries and the amount of fuel left in their tanks.
   c The mass of a roast beef and the time taken to cook it.
   d The height of Year 6 pupils and the number of brothers and sisters they have.
   e The number of customers in a supermarket over a week and the profit made by the supermarket that week.
   f The distance Year 11 pupils live from school and their exam results in English.
   g The amount of fertiliser a farmer sows and the amount of crops produced.

3 The table shows the Maths and Science results for eight pupils in Year 10.

Maths result	30	63	84	52	56	72	30	84
Science result	40	74	92	60	62	70	44	78

  a Draw a set of axes and plot the points on a scatter diagram, putting the Maths result along the horizontal axis.

  b Comment on the correlation.

  c Draw a line of best fit on your diagram.

  d Use your line of best fit to estimate the Science result for a pupil who scored 66 in their Maths test.

4 The table shows the engine size and average fuel consumption for eight cars in a showroom.

Engine size (cc)	1.4	2.0	1.8	1.5	2.0	1.1	1.2	1.6
Average fuel consumption (mpg)	52	38	41	47	27	60	56	50

  a Draw a set of axes and plot the points on a scatter diagram, putting the engine size along the horizontal axis.

  b Comment on the correlation.

  c Draw a line of best fit on your diagram.

  d Use your line of best fit to estimate the fuel consumption for a car that has an engine size of 1.9 cc.

  e Use your line of best fit to estimate the size of the engine in a car that has a fuel consumption of 45 mpg.

  f One of the points is an outlier. Circle this point on your diagram and explain why you think it is an outlier.

5 The table shows the heights and arm spans of 9 pupils in Year 11.

Height (cm)	144	155	169	158	174	182	172	150	140
Arm span (cm)	149	153	174	163	177	179	169	160	148

  a Draw a set of axes and plot the points on a scatter diagram, putting the height along the horizontal axis.

  b Comment on the correlation.

  c Draw a line of best fit on your diagram.

  d Use your line of best fit to estimate the arm span of a pupil who has a height of 163 cm.

  e Use your line of best fit to estimate the height of a pupil who has an arm span of 175 cm.

6 The table shows the average number of books read each month and the average number of hours spent watching TV each week by 10 adults.

Number of books	9	1	6	7	3	2	0	4	1	5
Hours watching TV	2	12	15	4	9	11	13	10	14	6

  a Draw a set of axes and plot the points on a scatter diagram, putting number of books along the horizontal axis.

  b Comment on the correlation.

  c Draw a line of best fit on your diagram.

  d Use your line of best fit to estimate the number of books read by an adult who watches 5 hours of TV each week.

  e There is one point which is an outlier. Put a circle around this point. Give a reason why this adult may stand out.

Exercise C

1 a Starting with $x = 1$ use the flow chart to fill in the table for values of x and T.

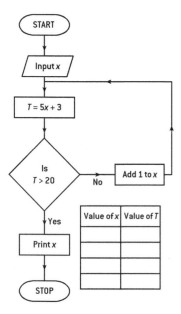

b What value is printed?

2 a Starting with $x = 1$ use the flow chart to fill in the table for values of x and A.

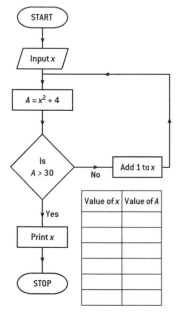

b What value is printed?

3 a Starting with $x = 1$ and $y = 1$ use the flow chart to fill in the table for values of x, y and P.

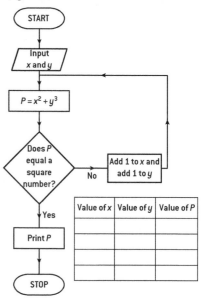

b What value is printed?

4 a Starting with $x = 2$ and $y = 2$ use the flow chart to fill in the table for values of x, y, C and D.

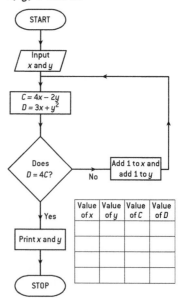

b What values are printed?

5 The table shows the frequency distribution for the heights of pupils in a Year 8 class.

Height (cm)	Frequency
$130 \leq h < 135$	1
$135 \leq h < 140$	3
$140 \leq h < 145$	4
$145 \leq h < 150$	7
$150 \leq h < 155$	5
$155 \leq h < 160$	3

    a Draw a frequency polygon to show this information.
    b How many pupils are in the class?

6 The table shows the frequency distribution for the weights of turkeys sold by a farmer at Christmas.

Weight (kg)	Frequency
$2 \leq w < 4$	3
$4 \leq w < 6$	11
$6 \leq w < 8$	22
$8 \leq w < 10$	18
$10 \leq w < 12$	7
$12 \leq w < 14$	3

    a Draw a frequency polygon to show this information.
    b How many turkeys did the farmer sell?

7 The table shows the frequency distribution for the times it took a group of people to complete a Maths challenge.

Time (minutes)	Frequency
$30 \leq t < 40$	5
$40 \leq t < 50$	9
$50 \leq t < 60$	23
$60 \leq t < 70$	18
$70 \leq t < 80$	11
$80 \leq t < 90$	4

    a Draw a frequency polygon to show this information.
    b How many people participated in the challenge?
    c What is the shortest possible time that someone could have taken to complete the challenge?

8   The table shows the frequency distribution for the distances 50 people travel to work.

Distance (km)	Frequency
$0 \leq d < 5$	8
$5 \leq d < 10$	6
$10 \leq d < 15$	11
$15 \leq d < 20$	14
$20 \leq d < 25$	8
$25 \leq d < 30$	3

a   Draw a frequency polygon to show this information.
b   What is the least distance someone could travel to work?

9   The table shows the frequency distribution for the actual weight of crisps in packets labelled 35 grams.

Weight (g)	Frequency
$33 \leq w < 34$	1
$34 \leq w < 35$	2
$35 \leq w < 36$	26
$36 \leq w < 37$	19
$37 \leq w < 38$	2

a   Draw a frequency polygon to show this information.
b   How many packets were sampled?
c   Would the crisp manufacturer be pleased with the results? Explain your answer.

10 The table shows the frequency distribution for the vital lung capacities of pupils in Year 12.

Vital lung capacity (litres)	Frequency girls	Frequency boys
$3.4 \leq x < 3.6$	3	2
$3.6 \leq x < 3.8$	7	5
$3.8 \leq x < 4.0$	26	24
$4.0 \leq x < 4.2$	17	25
$4.2 \leq x < 4.4$	4	7
$4.4 \leq x < 4.6$	1	3

a   Draw a frequency polygon to show the information for Year 12 boys.
b   On the same axes draw a frequency polygon to show the information for Year 12 girls.
c   How many pupils are there in Year 12?
d   Using the frequency polygons write down one comparison between the boys' and girls' lung capacities.

This chapter is about

■ recognising and extending number patterns, sequences and spatial arrangements
■ working out the inputs and outputs of simple function machines.

1 Look at the following

a Draw the next two patterns.
b Write down the number of dots in each pattern.
c What name is given to the numbers in this sequence?

2 Look at the following

a Draw the next two patterns.
b Write down the number of dots in each pattern.
c What name is given to the numbers in this sequence?

3 Look at the following.

Pattern 1   Pattern 2   Pattern 3

a Draw the next two patterns.
b Copy and complete the table.

Pattern number	1	2	3	4	5	6
Number of matchsticks						

4 Look at the following.

 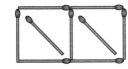 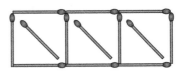

Pattern 1   Pattern 2   Pattern 3

a Draw the next two patterns.
b Copy and complete the table.

Pattern number	1	2	3	4	5	6
Number of matchsticks						

5 Look at the following pattern made from matchsticks.

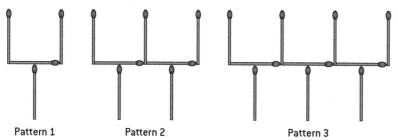

Pattern 1   Pattern 2   Pattern 3

a Draw the next two patterns.   **b** Copy and complete the table.

Pattern number	1	2	3	4	5	6
Number of matchsticks						

6 Find the output for each input in the following function machines.

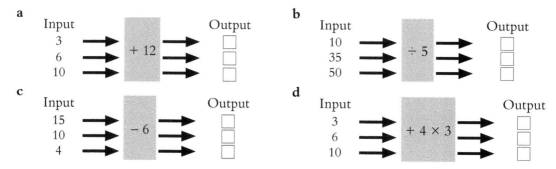

a
Input
3
6
10
$+ 12$
Output

b
Input
10
35
50
$\div 5$
Output

c
Input
15
10
4
$- 6$
Output

d
Input
3
6
10
$+ 4 \times 3$
Output

7 Work out the rules in each of the following function machines.

a
Input
6
8
9
Rule
Output
17
19
20

b
Input
30
63
72
Rule
Output
10
21
24

c
Input
2
5
8
Rule
Output
7
16
25

d
Input
5
7
10
Rule
Output
17
25
37

8 Find the input for each output in the following function machines.

a
Input
$\times 2$
Output
12
20
26

b
Input
$+ 7$
Output
11
7
3

c
Input
$\div 7$
Output
4
15
32

d
Input
$- 2 \times 3$
Output
12
24
51

CHAPTER 30

Pythagoras' theorem

This chapter is about

- stating Pythagoras' theorem
- using Pythagoras' theorem to find missing sides in right-angled triangles
- applying Pythagoras' theorem to solve problems in 2D.

1 For each triangle state Pythagoras' theorem in terms of the letters given.

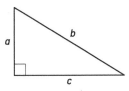

a

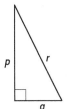

b

c

d

2 For each triangle find the length of the lettered side, giving your answer to 2 decimal places where necessary.

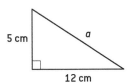

a

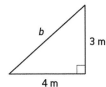

b

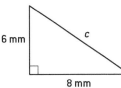

c

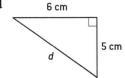

d

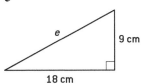

e

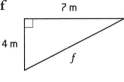

f

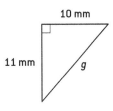

g

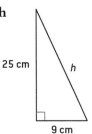

h

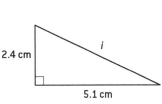

i

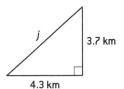

j

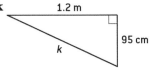

k

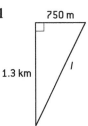

l

3 For each triangle find the length of the lettered side, giving your answer to 2 decimal places where necessary.

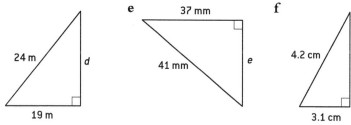

a

a 15 cm

9 cm

b 20 m

b 25 m

c

14 cm 5 cm

c

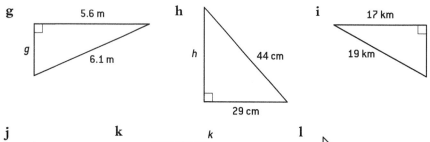

d

24 m *d*

19 m

e 37 mm

41 mm *e*

f

4.2 cm *f*

3.1 cm

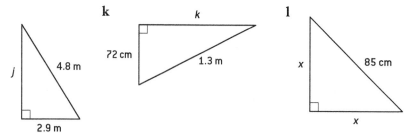

g 5.6 m

g 6.1 m

h

h 44 cm

29 cm

i 17 km

19 km *i*

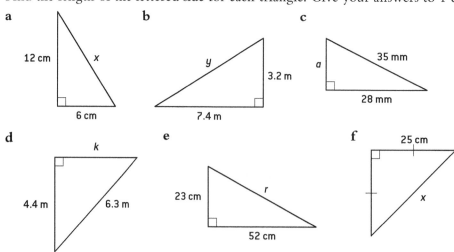

j

j 4.8 m

2.9 m

k *k*

72 cm 1.3 m

l

x 85 cm

x

4 Find the length of the lettered side for each triangle. Give your answers to 1 decimal place.

a

12 cm *x*

6 cm

b

y 3.2 m

7.4 m

c

a 35 mm

28 mm

d

k

4.4 m 6.3 m

e

23 cm *r*

52 cm

f 25 cm

x

5 Dylan walked diagonally across a school playing field when collecting in the corner flags. How far does he walk from corner A to corner C?

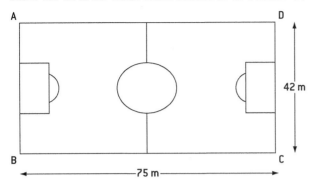

6 Gavin says that he has drawn a right-angled triangle. The sides are 5 cm, 12 cm and 15 cm. Is he correct? Explain your answer.

7 A ladder is placed on horizontal ground and leans against a vertical wall. It reaches a height of 6 m up the wall. The foot of the ladder is 2.5 m from the wall. Calculate the length of the ladder.

8 A rectangle has length 24 cm and width 7 cm. Find the length of one of its diagonals.

9 Calculate the area of the isosceles triangle below.

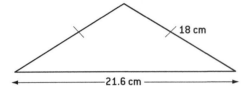

10 William is making a gate with three horizontal lengths, three vertical lengths and one diagonal length as shown. Work out the total length of timber he needs to make the gate.

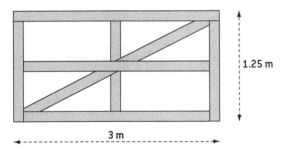

11 Find the perimeter of this trapezium.

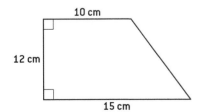

CHAPTER 31 Bearings

This chapter is about

- knowing how to calculate, measure and draw bearings.

1 Work out the bearing of **Q from P** in each of the following. The diagrams are not drawn accurately.

a

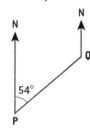

b

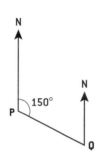

c

d

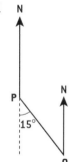

e

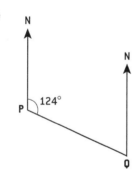

f

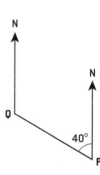

g

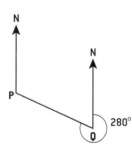

h

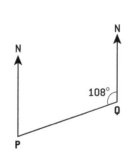

i

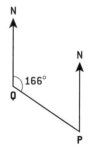

2 Work out the bearing of **P from Q** in each of the diagrams in question 1.

3 The bearing of M from T is 043°. What is the bearing of T from M?

4 The bearing of A from B is 161°. What is the bearing of B from A?

5 The bearing of D from C is 235°. What is the bearing of C from D?

6 Draw and label each of the following three-figure bearings. In each case assume that North is parallel to the margin in your exercise book.

    a Mark P on your page. Draw Q 5 cm from P on a bearing of 075°.
    b Mark X on your page. Draw Y 4 cm from X on a bearing of 140°.
    c Mark M on your page. Draw N 6 cm from M on a bearing of 163°.
    d Mark R on your page. Draw S 5 cm from R on a bearing of 235°.

7 Use an angle measurer or a protractor to find the bearing of

    a A from B   **b** C from D   **c** E from F.

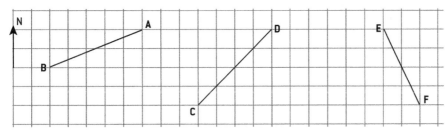

8 Draw the points P and Q which are 6 cm apart horizontally.

    P ——————— 6 cm ——————— Q

R is on a bearing of 060° from P. R is on a bearing of 320° from Q.

    a Locate the position of R.
    b Measure the length of PR.

9 A hiker walks 2 km due South from a starting point S. She then walks 3.5 km on a bearing of 120° to point L where she stops for lunch.
    a Using a scale of 1 cm = 1 km construct a scale drawing of the hiker's journey.
    b Use your drawing to find
        i the direct distance from S to L
        ii the bearing of S from L.

CHAPTER 32

Perimeter, area and volume

This chapter is about

- knowing the meaning of perimeter, area and volume
- calculating the perimeter of a square, a rectangle and a triangle
- knowing and using the formula for the area of a rectangle or a square
- knowing and using the formula for the area of a triangle
- calculating the volume of a cube and a cuboid
- calculating the volume of a prism.

Exercise A

1 Find the perimeter of each of the following shapes. State the units.

a
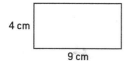
4 cm
9 cm

b
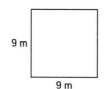
9 m
9 m

c
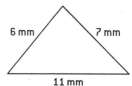
6 mm   7 mm
11 mm

d
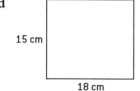
15 cm
18 cm

e
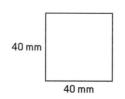
40 mm
40 mm

f
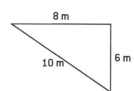
8 m
10 m   6 m

g
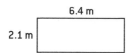
6.4 m
2.1 m

h
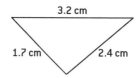
3.2 cm
1.7 cm   2.4 cm

i
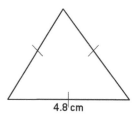
4.8 cm

j
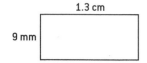
1.3 cm
9 mm

k
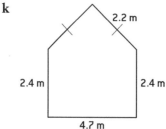
2.2 m
2.4 m   2.4 m
4.7 m

l
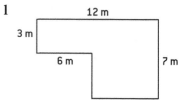
12 m
3 m
6 m   7 m

2 The perimeter of a square is 20 cm. Find the length of each of its sides.

3 The perimeter of a rectangle is 34 cm. The length is 10 cm. Find the breadth.

4 The perimeter of an equilateral triangle is 48 cm. Find the length of each side.

5 The perimeter of a kite is 60 cm. Given that one of the sides is 18 cm, find the lengths of the other three sides.

6 The perimeter of an isosceles triangle is 72 cm. Given that one of the sides is 30 cm, work out the lengths of the other sides of two possible triangles with this perimeter.

7 Find the area of each of the following shapes. State the units.

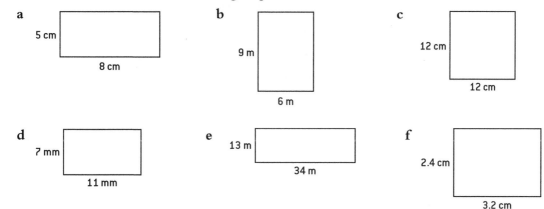

8 Find the area of a square with side 11 cm.

9 Find the area of a rectangle with length 6 mm and breadth 4 mm.

10 Find the area of a square with side 20 m.

11 Find the area of a rectangle with length 8.4 mm and breadth 3 mm.

12 Find the area of a rectangle with length 4.2 cm and breadth 30 mm.

13 Find the area of each triangle.

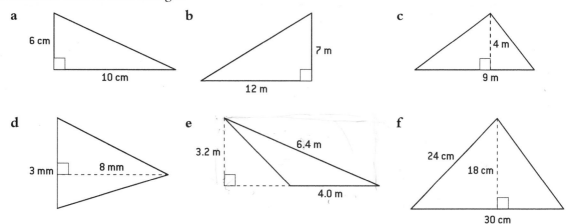

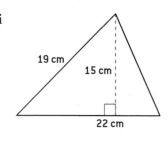

g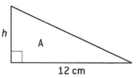

14 Find the area of a triangle with base 8 cm and perpendicular height 12 cm.

15 Find the area of a triangle with base 10 m and perpendicular height 17 m.

16 Find the area of a triangle with base 6 cm and perpendicular height 2.5 cm.

17 Find the area of a triangle with base 20 mm and perpendicular height 38 mm.

18 Find the area of a triangle with base 2.4 cm and perpendicular height 6 cm.

19 A rectangle has area 30 cm². Its length is 6 cm. What is its breadth?

20 A rectangle has area 18 cm². Write down the length and breadth of four different rectangles with this area.

21 A square has area 64 cm². What is the length of each of its sides?

22 A square has area 36 m². What is its perimeter?

23 The triangle A has area 30 cm². Find h.

24 A square has perimeter 28 cm. What is its area?

25 A rectangle has area 12 cm². Write down 3 possible values for the perimeter of this rectangle.

Exercise B

1 Find the volume of each solid. State the units.

a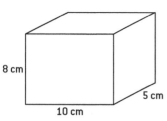

b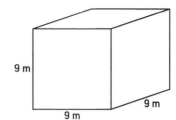

c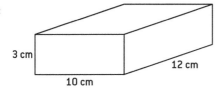

d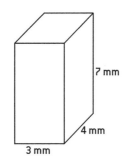

2 Find the volume of each of the given cuboids, stating the correct units.

  a length = 6 cm, breadth = 5 cm, height = 4 cm
  b length = 3 mm, breadth = 8 mm, height = 10 mm
  c length = 2.5 m, breadth = 2 m, height = 9 m
  d length = 8 cm, breadth = 6 cm, height = 20 mm
  e length = 3 m, breadth = 60 cm, height = 15 cm

3 Calculate the volume of a cube with edge 2 cm.

4 Calculate the volume of a cube with edge 12 mm.

5 Calculate the volume of a cube with edge 3.2 m.

6 A cube has volume 1000 cm³. What is the length of each edge?

7 A cube has volume 125 cm³. What is the length of each edge?

8 A cube has volume 8 m³. What is the total length of all its edges?

9 A cuboid has volume 48 cm³. The length is 6 cm and the height is 2 cm. What is the breadth?

10 A cuboid has volume 60 cm³. Copy and complete the table giving four different sets of possible dimensions for this cuboid.

Cuboid	Length	Breadth	Height	Volume
1				60 cm³
2				60 cm³
3				60 cm³
4				60 cm³

11 Calculate the volume of each triangular prism.

  a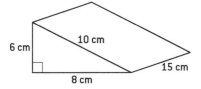

  b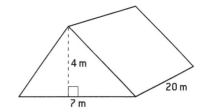

Expanding brackets

This chapter is about

■ multiplying a bracket by a single term
■ expanding and simplifying algebraic expressions involving brackets.

1 Expand each of the following.

  a $3(x + 2)$ **b** $5(y + 4)$
  c $2(t + 5)$ **d** $6(5 + p)$
  e $4(3 + x)$ **f** $9(3 + v)$
  g $4(3x + 5)$ **h** $5(2 + 2n)$
  i $4(e + 2f)$ **j** $10(2x + 3w)$
  k $5(3g + 2h)$ **l** $7(3a + 5b)$

2 Multiply out each of the following.

  a $4(x - 3)$ **b** $5(d - 2)$
  c $3(y - 3)$ **d** $5(6 - t)$
  e $9(2 - x)$ **f** $11(5 - p)$
  g $2(3x - 2)$ **h** $4(2g - 1)$
  i $7(4v - 9)$ **j** $6(3 - 2x)$
  k $6(8x - 7y)$ **l** $5(2w - 3e)$

3 Expand each of the following.

  a $-2(x + 3)$ **b** $-4(y + 2)$
  c $-5(m + c)$ **d** $-3(t + 2y)$
  e $-8(2f + 3g)$ **f** $-6(5x + 6y)$
  g $-2(t - 4)$ **h** $-9(a - 3)$
  i $-3(v - 7)$ **j** $-5(4 - 3w)$
  k $-11(7x - 8y)$ **l** $-6(2m - 9n)$

4 Multiply out each of the following.

  a $x(x + 4)$ **b** $y(y + 5)$
  c $m(m + 3)$ **d** $e(3 - e)$
  e $t(t - 4)$ **f** $a(a - 5)$
  g $x(y + x)$ **h** $m(9 - m)$
  i $c(c + d)$ **j** $d(5 - d)$
  k $x(x^2 + 4)$ **l** $w(w - 2n)$

5 Expand and simplify each of the following.

a $5(x + 2) + 3x$ **b** $4(x + 3) + 5x$

c $7(x + 1) - 4x$ **d** $3(4y + 2) - 5y$

e $3(y + 2) + 4(y + 1)$ **f** $2(y + 5) + 3(y + 2)$

g $5(c + 2) + 2(c - 3)$ **h** $4(d + 3) + 3(d - 4)$

i $2(m - 1) + 4(m + 2)$ **j** $5(e - 2) + 3(e - 3)$

k $4(x + 7) + 3(2x - 3)$ **l** $8(a - 3) + 5(3a - 3)$

m $6(x + 2) - 3(x + 2)$ **n** $2(x - 1) - 4(x + 2)$

o $3(2x + 5y) + 4(x - 2y)$ **p** $5(x - 2y) + 3(2x - y)$

q $4(2x - 3y) - 2(3x - 2y)$ **r** $t(t + 3) - t(t - 4)$

s $m(m - 5) + 2(m - 2)$ **t** $x(4 + x) - x(2 + x)$

u $y(10 - y) + y(3 - y)$ **v** $5(2x + y) - (3x - 2y)$

w $3(2x - 3y + c) - 2(x - 4y + 2c)$ **x** $a(3b + 4c) - b(2a - 3)$

6 Match each rectangle to its correct area.

a

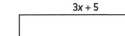

3x + 5

4

      i $3x + 20$

      ii $12x + 20$

      iii $7x + 9$

b

5a – 3

2a

      i $10a - 6$

      ii $10a^2 - 6$

      iii $10a^2 - 6a$

This chapter is about

- finding the term-to-term rule of a number sequence
- generating terms of number sequences using term-to-term rules.

1 For each sequence
  i   write down the next two terms
  ii write down the rule.

  a 7, 10, 13, 16, …   b 5, 10, 20, 40, …
  c 30, 24, 18, 12, …   d 20, 31, 42, 53, …
  e 50 000, 5000, 500, 50, …   f 42, 37, 32, 27, …
  g 3, 60, 1200, 24 000, …   h 0.2, 0.4, 0.6, 0.8, …

2 For each sequence
  i   find the missing terms
  ii write down the rule.

  a 37, 33, ___, 25, ___, 17   b 11, 19, ___, 35, ___, 51
  c ___, 3, 9, ___, 81, 243   d ___, 12, 24, ___, 96, ___
  e 60, ___, ___, 15, ___   f ___, ___, 80, 800, 8000
  g 0.64, 0.72, ___, 0.88, 0.96, ___ h ___, 500, 250, 125, ___

3 Work out the first five terms in each sequence. You are given the first term and the rule.

	First term	Rule	Sequence
Example	5	× 3	5, 15, 45, 135, 405
a	6	+ 10	
b	40	− 6	
c	11	× 2	
d	1200	÷ 2	
e	3.6	+ 0.2	
f	3	× 2 and + 1	
g	2	+ 3 and × 2	
h	10	− 5 and × 3	
i	40	÷ 2 and + 4	
j	1	× 6 and + 2	

4 In a sequence the rule is 'add 5'. The third term is 17.

  a What is the fourth term?
  b What is the first term?
  c What is the eighth term?

5 In a sequence the rule is 'subtract 3 and multiply by 2'. The second term is 12.

  a What is the third term?
  b What is the first term?
  c What is the sixth term?

CHAPTER 35

Symmetry and transformations

This chapter is about

- knowing what is meant by symmetry, line symmetry and rotational symmetry
- giving the number of lines of symmetry for any shape
- giving the order of rotational symmetry for any shape
- knowing the properties of a reflection, rotation, translation and an enlargement
- drawing the image of a shape after each of these transformations
- finding the original shape given the image and the transformation
- describing fully the transformation given the original shape and its image

Exercise A

1   Copy each shape onto squared paper and draw on all the lines of symmetry.

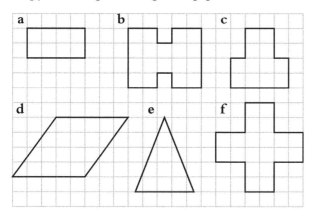

2   Copy each of the following parts of shapes and the lines of symmetry onto squared paper. Complete each shape.

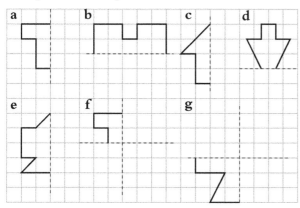

3 Copy each pattern below and add **two** squares to each pattern so that it has

    a 1 line of symmetry   **b** 2 lines of symmetry   **c** 4 lines of symmetry.

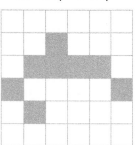 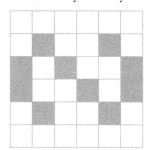 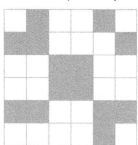

4 For each of the following state whether the shape has rotational symmetry or not. If it does have rotational symmetry, state the order.

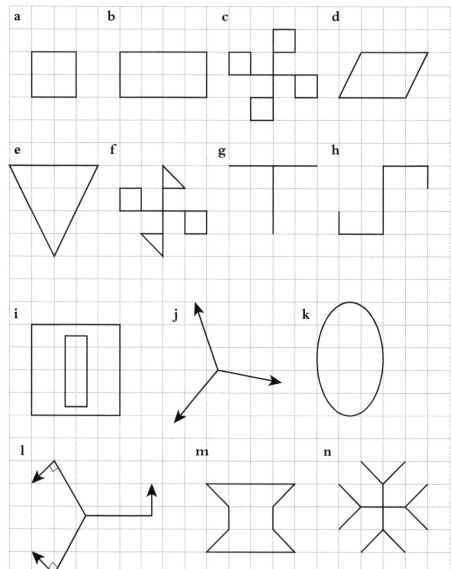

5 Copy each pattern below and add **two** squares to each pattern so that it has
  a rotational symmetry order 2
  b rotational symmetry order 4.

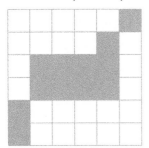

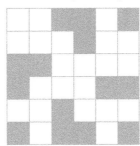

6 a Write down the name of the triangle which has 3 lines of symmetry and rotational symmetry order 3.
  b Write down the names of 2 quadrilaterals which have 2 lines of symmetry and rotational symmetry order 2.
  c Write down the name of a shape which has 5 lines of symmetry and rotational symmetry order 5.
  d Write down the name of a quadrilateral which has no lines of symmetry and rotational symmetry order 2.
  e Write down the name of a shape which has 8 lines of symmetry and rotational symmetry order 8.

Exercise B

1 Copy the grid below and object A onto squared paper.

  a Reflect object A in the *y*-axis and label it B.

  b Reflect object A in the *x*-axis and label it C.

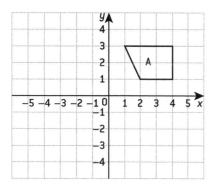

2 Copy the grid below and object D onto squared paper.

  a Reflect object D in the line *y* = 1 and label the image E.

  b Reflect object D in the line *x* = −1 and label the image F.

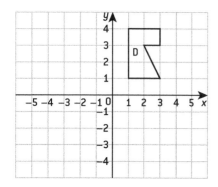

3 Copy the grid below and object G onto squared paper.

  a Reflect object G in the line *y* = −2 and label the image H.

  b Reflect object G in the line *x* = −1 and label the image I.

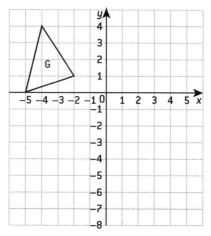

4 Describe fully the single transformation that maps

  a A onto B   **b** A onto C

  c A onto D   **d** D onto I

  e D onto G   **f** G onto F

  g E onto F   **h** C onto E

  i G onto H.

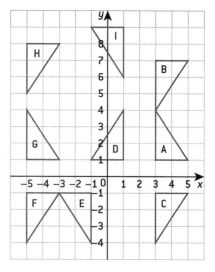

Exercise C

1 Copy the grid and object A onto squared paper.
   a Rotate object A 90° clockwise about the origin. Label the image B.
   b Rotate object A 90° anticlockwise about (0, 1). Label the image C.

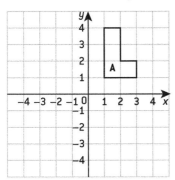

2 Copy the grid and object D onto squared paper.
   a Rotate object D 90° clockwise about (2, 0). Label the image E.
   b Rotate object D 90° anticlockwise about (−1, 0). Label the image F.

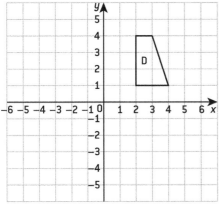

3 Copy the grid and object G onto squared paper.
   a Rotate object G 180° about (0, 0). Label the image H.
   b Rotate object G 90° anticlockwise about (1, 1). Label the image I.

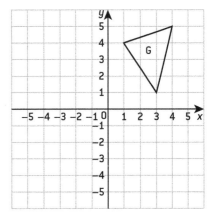

4 Fully describe the single transformation that maps
   a A onto B   b A onto C
   c A onto D   d A onto E
   e A onto F   f A onto G
   g A onto H   h A onto I.

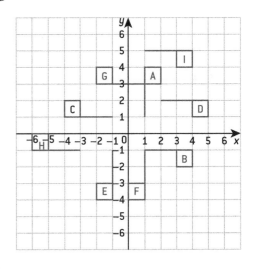

Exercise D

1 Write down in words the translation described by each of the following column vectors.

a $\begin{pmatrix} 2 \\ 3 \end{pmatrix}$ b $\begin{pmatrix} 5 \\ -4 \end{pmatrix}$ c $\begin{pmatrix} 0 \\ 6 \end{pmatrix}$ d $\begin{pmatrix} -5 \\ 2 \end{pmatrix}$ e $\begin{pmatrix} 5 \\ 0 \end{pmatrix}$ f $\begin{pmatrix} -3 \\ -1 \end{pmatrix}$

2 Write down a column vector that is equivalent to the translations described.
  a 3 right and 5 up   b 4 left and 4 down   c 1 right and 5 down
  d 9 to the right   e 6 down   f 15 right and 10 down
  g 13 left and 11 up   h 7 up   i 24 to the left

3 Copy the grid and object T onto squared paper.

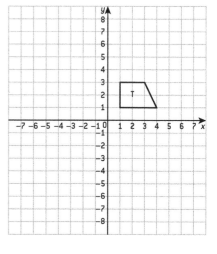

  a Translate object T 2 right and 3 up. Label the image A.
  b Translate object T 3 left and 3 up. Label the image B.
  c Translate object T 1 left and 2 down. Label the image C.
  d Translate object T 5 left and 5 down. Label the image D.

  e Translate object T $\begin{pmatrix} 3 \\ -1 \end{pmatrix}$. Label the image E.

  f Translate object T $\begin{pmatrix} -6 \\ -1 \end{pmatrix}$. Label the image F.

  g Translate object T $\begin{pmatrix} 2 \\ -5 \end{pmatrix}$. Label the image G.

  h Translate object T $\begin{pmatrix} -6 \\ 2 \end{pmatrix}$. Label the image H.

4 Describe the translation that maps A onto the images B to J. Give your answers using column vector notation.

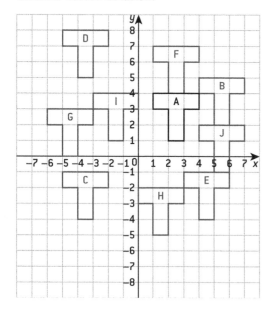

Exercise E

1 Copy the grid and object A onto squared paper.
  a Enlarge object A by a scale factor 2, centre of enlargement (0, 0). Label the image B.
  b Enlarge object A by a scale factor 2, centre of enlargement (3, 1). Label the image C.
  c Enlarge object A by a scale factor 2, centre of enlargement (2, 4). Label the image D.

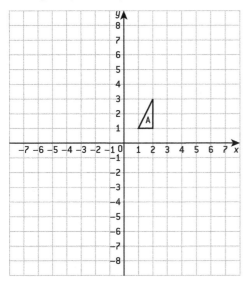

2 Copy the grid and object A onto squared paper.
  a Enlarge object A by a scale factor 3, centre of enlargement (−2, 1). Label the image B.
  b Enlarge object A by a scale factor 3, centre of enlargement (−1, 3). Label the image C.

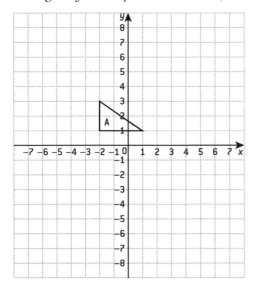

3 Copy the grid and object E onto squared paper.
  a Enlarge object E by a scale factor 3, centre of enlargement (−4, −5). Label the image F.
  b Enlarge object E by a scale factor 2, centre of enlargement (−1, −3). Label the image G.

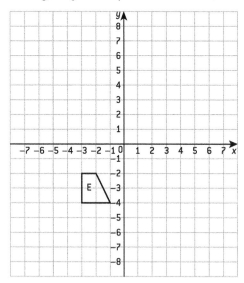

4 Describe fully the single transformation which maps
  a A to B   **b** A to C   **c** A to D   **d** B to D.

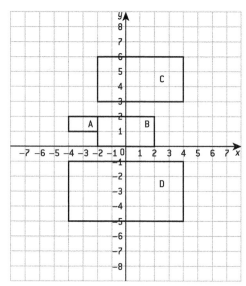

Exercise F

1 Describe fully the single transformation which maps

   a A to B   **b** A to C   **c** B to D   **d** D to E

   e A to F   **f** C to G   **g** D to H   **h** H to F

   i I to C   **j** G to J.

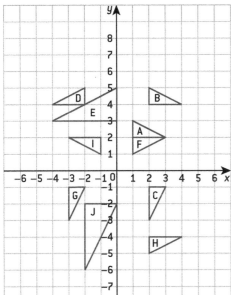

2 Describe fully the single transformation which maps

   a P to Q   **b** Q to R   **c** P to S   **d** T to P

   e R to U   **f** V to S   **g** S to W   **h** R to X.

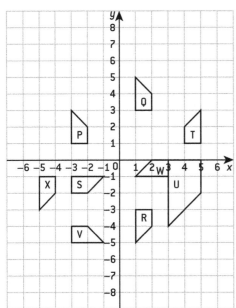

CHAPTER 36

Brackets and factorising

> **This chapter is about**
>
> ■ factorising algebraic expressions.

1 Factorise each expression.

a	$2w + 10$	**b**	$3m + 12$
c	$5y - 20$	**d**	$2e - 14$
e	$6m + 3$	**f**	$15d + 20$
g	$30g - 12$	**h**	$16i - 20$
i	$18n + 27$	**j**	$6 - 24c$
k	$20i + 30f$	**l**	$7x + 21y$
m	$9m - 36n$	**n**	$12e + 18g$
o	$40j + 36k$	**p**	$8p - 16q$
q	$21h - 28e$	**r**	$4t + 32k$
s	$60i - 12m$	**t**	$30w + 15e$
u	$45x - 30y$		

2 Factorise each expression.

a	$5x + xy$	**b**	$4e - et$
c	$2g - gn$	**d**	$10i + im$
e	$h + hx$	**f**	$3w - cw$
g	$y^2 + y$	**h**	$e^2 + 3e$
i	$h - h^2$	**j**	$x + 5x^2$
k	$w + 2wn$	**l**	$5c - c^2$
m	$m + m^3$	**n**	$7d^2 - 3d$
o	$5e^2 - 4eh$	**p**	$6fg - 5f$
q	$3xy + 5ex$	**r**	$8x^2 - 5xt$
s	$2mk - 3k^2$	**t**	$7bc - 4b^2$
u	$abc + cde$		

3 Fully factorise each expression.

a	$3xe + 6xy$	**b**	$15wc - 5wd$
c	$8ey + 12e$	**d**	$6mc + 10m$
e	$10ey + 25y$	**f**	$9hy - 12h$
g	$20ix - 30i$	**h**	$8xy + 4x$
i	$20cd - 5c$	**j**	$7e - 14ey$
k	$3d^2 + 9dy$	**l**	$6xy + 2y^2$
m	$12mf - 6m^2$	**n**	$15x^2 + 10xy$
o	$16n^2 - 8en$	**p**	$30iy - 40i^2$
q	$4e^3 - 4en$	**r**	$6xy - 3x^3$
s	$10wc + 8w^2 - 6w$	**t**	$10x^2 + 5xy - 15x^3$
u	$8ab + 12b^2 - 4bc$		

CHAPTER 37 Circles

This chapter is about

- calculating the circumference of a circle and the perimeter of shapes including parts of circles
- calculating the area of a circle or shapes including parts of circles
- calculating the volume of a cylinder or semicircular prism.

Exercise A

1 Work out the circumference of each circle. Use π = 3.14

a
6 cm

b
14 cm

c
7.5 m

d
11.4 m

2 Work out the circumference of each circle. Use π on your calculator. Round answers to 2 decimal places.

a
21 cm

b
8.6 mm

c
43 cm

d
43 cm

3 A circle has radius 6 cm. Find: **a** its diameter **b** its circumference to 1 decimal place.

4 A circle has diameter 11 cm. Find: **a** its radius **b** its circumference to 1 decimal place.

5 The circumference of a circle is 40 cm. Find its diameter correct to 2 decimal places.

6 The circumference of a circle is 65 cm. Find its radius correct to 2 decimal places.

7 Find the perimeter of each shape. Use π = 3.14

a
24 cm

b
16 cm

c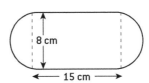
8 cm
15 cm

d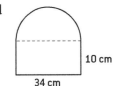
10 cm
34 cm

8 A car wheel has diameter 60 cm. It makes 1000 revolutions on a journey. What distance in km does it cover?

9 The wheel of a tractor has diameter 1.6 m. How many complete revolutions will it make when it covers a distance of 320 m?

Circles 95

Exercise B

1 Work out the area of each circle. Use π = 3.14

a   6 cm

b   2.5 m

c   14 cm

d   11.4 m

2 Work out the area of each circle. Use π on your calculator. Round your answers to 2 decimal places.

a   9 cm

b   3.6 mm

c   15 cm

d   1.84 m

3 A circle has radius 8 cm. Using π = 3.14 find its area correct to 2 decimal places.

4 A circle has diameter 13 m. Using π = 3.14 find its area correct to 2 decimal places.

5 The area of a circle is 59 cm². Find its radius correct to 1 decimal place.

6 The area of a circle is 230 m². Find its radius correct to 2 decimal places.

7 The area of a circle is 34 cm². Find its diameter correct to 1 decimal place.

8 Find the area of each shape. Use π = 3.14

a   36 cm

b   14 cm

c 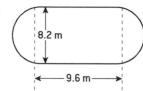 8.2 m   9.6 m

d 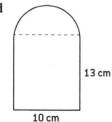 13 cm   10 cm

e 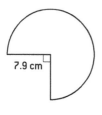 7.9 cm

9 Find the shaded area in each of the following.
Use π = 3.14

a A square of side 3 cm is cut from a circle of radius 5 cm.

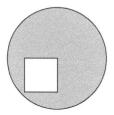

b A semicircle is cut from a rectangle.

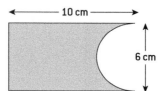

10 cm   6 cm

c The diameter of the outer circle is 18 cm.
The diameter of the inner circle is 14 cm.

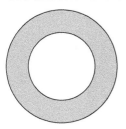

e The diameter of the large semicircle is 24 cm.

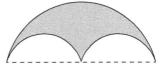

d The diameter of the large circle is 20 cm.
The three small circles each have
diameter 3 cm.

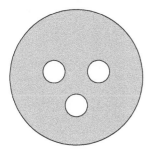

Exercise C

1 A circle has radius 8 cm. Find:
   a its diameter   **b** its circumference   **c** its area.

2 A circle has diameter 25 cm. Find:
   a its radius   **b** its circumference   **c** its area.

3 A circle has circumference 16 cm. Find its area.

4 A circle has area 92 cm². Find its circumference.

5 This semicircle has area 35 cm².

Find its perimeter.

6 This quadrant has area 120 m².

Find its perimeter.

7 Jennifer puts a ribbon around the edge of a circular cloth. There is a 5 cm overlap of ribbon.
The length of the ribbon is 70 cm. What is the area of the circular cloth?

8 Find the volume of each cylinder in cm³. Use π = 3.14

a
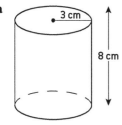
3 cm
8 cm

b
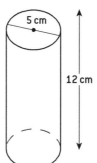
5 cm
12 cm

c
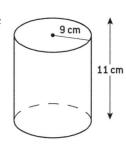
9 cm
11 cm

d
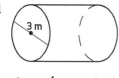
3 m
4 m

9 A tin of beans has diameter 7 cm and height 10.5 cm. Work out its capacity.

10 Find the capacity of each cylinder in litres. Use π = 3.14

a
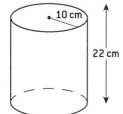
10 cm
22 cm

b
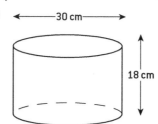
30 cm
18 cm

c
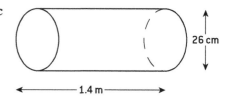
26 cm
1.4 m

11 A cylinder has volume 900 cm³ and radius 6 cm. Find its height.

12 A cylinder has volume 550 cm³ and diameter 8.4 cm. Find its height.

13 A cylinder has volume 825 cm³ and height 25 cm. Find its radius.

14 A cylinder has capacity 6 litres and radius 8 cm. Find its height.

15 A cylinder has capacity 1.75 litres and height 6.5 cm. Find its radius.

16 Cylinder A has radius 5 cm and height 10 cm. Cylinder B has radius 8 cm and height 22 cm. How many times bigger is the capacity of cylinder B than the capacity of cylinder A?

17 Due to EU legislation, a farmer has a slurry store full to capacity. The store holds 550 000 litres. The farmer's son Harry-James is using a slurry tanker to empty the store. The diameter of the slurry tanker is 160 cm and its length is 340 cm. How many **full** tanker loads can Harry-James remove when emptying the store?

This chapter is about

- knowing what a ratio is
- knowing how to simplify a ratio
- finding equivalent ratios
- using ratios to calculate amounts.

1 There are 5 red, 4 black and 3 green sweets in a bag. Write down the ratio of
  a red : green   **b** green : red   **c** black : red
  d red : green : black   **e** black : green : red

2 Write each ratio in its lowest terms.
  a 4 : 8   **b** 15 : 10   **c** 12 : 16   **d** 45 : 30
  e 20 : 24   **f** 21 : 30   **g** 32 : 40   **h** 28 : 35
  i 90 : 15   **j** 80 : 86   **k** 36 : 63   **l** 24 : 48 : 40

3 Write each of the following as a ratio in its simplest form.
  a 20p to £3   **b** 50p to £4.50   **c** 2 m to 40 cm   **d** 6 mm to 4 cm
  e 5 km to 800 m   **f** 40 mins to 1 hr   **g** £1.80 to £4.20   **h** 4 mins to 50 secs
  i 7.5 m to 25 cm   **j** 6.4 kg to 4.8 kg   **k** 0.4 L to 240 ml   **l** 3 cm to 0.6 mm

4 Find the missing values for each pair of equal ratios.
  a 2 : 5   **b** 5 : 8   **c** 6 : 7   **d** 9 : 10
  □ : 20   30 : □   □ : 49   54 : □

  e 2 : 3 : 7   **f** 3 : 7 : 8   **g** 2 : □ : 9   **h** □ : 5 : 12
  16 : □ : □   □ : □ : 40   □ : 63 : 81   6 : 30 : □

5 The ratio of males to females at a gym is 4 : 5. There are 20 females at the gym. How many males are at the gym?

6 The ratio of sugar to butter in a recipe is 3 : 8. Elaine uses 60 g of sugar. How much butter does she need to use?

7 The ratio of the length of a rectangle to its breadth is 9 : 4. The length is 72 cm. What is the area of the rectangle?

8 The ratio of blue paint to yellow paint to make a particular shade of green is 7 : 2. Walt uses 140 ml of blue paint.
  a How much yellow paint does he use in the mixture?
  b How much green paint does he have?

9 Kieran, Peter and Thomas each donate money to the same charity in the ratio 2 : 5 : 10. Peter donated £40.
  How much did the three boys donate altogether?

10 Gillian mixes orange juice and water in the ratio 3 : 10. She uses 90 ml of orange juice. How much of the mixture does she have in the jug?

11 Rachel and Aimee share sweets in the ratio 5 : 4.
  Rachel gives half of her sweets to her brother.
  Given that Rachel has 15 sweets left, work out how many sweets Aimee received.

12 The ratio of boys to girls in a class is $4:5$.
  a What fraction of the pupils are girls?
  b What fraction of the pupils are boys?

13 The ratio of red sweets to green sweets in a bag is $7:1$.
  a What fraction of the sweets are green?
  b What fraction of the sweets are red?

14 Ruby, Steve and Tom share money in the ratio $4:3:5$.
  a What fraction of the money does Tom receive?
  b What fraction of the money does Ruby receive?

15 In a nursery class, $\frac{1}{4}$ of the pupils are girls. Write down the ratio of girls:boys in its simplest form.

16 In a car showroom, $\frac{3}{5}$ of the cars are hatchbacks. The rest of the cars are saloons. Write down the ratio of hatchbacks to saloons in its simplest form.

17 In a garden, $\frac{4}{7}$ of the area is lawn. The rest is patio. Write down the ratio of patio to lawn in its simplest form.

CHAPTER 39 Equations 2

This chapter is about

- solving linear equations involving fractional variables
- solving linear equations involving brackets
- solving linear equations with the variable on both sides of the equation
- writing linear equations
- using trial and improvement to solve equations that cannot be solved by simple analytical methods.

Exercise A

1 Solve each of the following equations.

a $x + 8 = 11$	**b** $y - 7 = 5$	**c** $3d = 12$
d $\frac{x}{2} = 8$	**e** $2c + 3 = 15$	**f** $4m - 1 = 19$
g $3g + 2 = 11$	**h** $5h - 6 = 14$	**i** $2x + 5 = 21$
j $10c - 4 = 26$	**k** $y + 7 = 2$	**l** $d - 3 = -6$
m $2x = -14$	**n** $3e = -30$	**o** $2x = 7$
p $9h = 5$	**q** $2w + 7 = 1$	**r** $3t - 4 = 7$
s $3m - 3 = -8$	**t** $5x + 1 = -3$	**u** $4y + 2 = -12$
v $7x - 4 = -1$	**w** $3x + 4 = 4$	**x** $5p - 9 = -7$

2 Solve each of the following equations.

a $\frac{x}{2} + 5 = 9$	**b** $\frac{m}{5} - 2 = 5$	**c** $\frac{c}{4} + 3 = 11$
d $\frac{w}{3} - 6 = 2$	**e** $\frac{d}{10} - 1 = 9$	**f** $\frac{y}{8} + 3 = 5$
g $\frac{x}{5} - 3 = 3$	**h** $4 + \frac{e}{6} = 8$	**i** $10 + \frac{h}{2} = 16$
j $\frac{x}{3} - 4 = -2$	**k** $\frac{t}{4} - 10 = -3$	**l** $\frac{c}{5} + 8 = 2$
m $\frac{n}{3} + 5 = 1$	**n** $\frac{r}{2} - 3 = -7$	**o** $\frac{t}{6} - 4 = -8$
p $\frac{x}{3} + 2 = -3$	**q** $\frac{y}{4} + 5 = -3$	**r** $\frac{d}{2} + 12 = 5$
s $\frac{t}{7} - 6 = -3$	**t** $\frac{b}{5} + 4 = -5$	**u** $\frac{c}{3} - 6 = -2$
v $\frac{x}{10} - 6 = 6$	**w** $\frac{x}{2} + 3 = 3$	**x** $\frac{p}{9} - 4 = -9$

3 Solve each of the following equations.

a $8 - 2x = 2$	**b** $5 - 3x = 11$	**c** $10 - 4x = 22$
d $14 - 2x = 8$	**e** $8 - 5x = 3$	**f** $18 - 6x = 6$
g $34 - 4x = 6$	**h** $11 - 3x = 2$	**i** $37 - 7x = 9$

j $7 - \dfrac{x}{3} = 2$ **k** $10 - \dfrac{x}{5} = 12$ **l** $3 - \dfrac{x}{2} = 1$

m $10 - \dfrac{x}{4} = 20$ **n** $7 - \dfrac{x}{10} = 3$ **o** $8 - \dfrac{x}{2} = 9$

p $23 - 6x = 5$ **q** $6 - \dfrac{x}{8} = 3$ **r** $36 - 11x = 3$

s $11 - \dfrac{x}{5} = 4$ **t** $58 - 8x = 10$ **u** $11 - \dfrac{x}{2} = -4$

v $8 - 3x = -7$ **w** $2 - \dfrac{x}{2} = -4$ **x** $6 - 7x = 13$

4 Solve each of the following equations.

a $2(x + 1) = 8$	**b** $3(y - 2) = 15$	**c** $5(w - 3) = 35$
d $2(4m - 1) = 6$	**e** $3(2e + 5) = 27$	**f** $4(3g - 2) = 28$
g $2(x - 1) = 13$	**h** $3(d - 2) = 5$	**i** $5(n - 1) = 1$
j $2(4t - 3) = 5$	**k** $4(2 + 3c) = 11$	**l** $3(5 + y) = 16$
m $2(x + 3) = 4$	**n** $5(m + 4) = 5$	**o** $3(w + 8) = 12$
p $6(p + 1) = 6$	**q** $2(3y + 2) = 1$	**r** $9(x + 2) = 0$
s $5(t - 7) = 15$	**t** $3(x - 4) + 2x = 3$	**u** $4(x + 2) + 2x = 20$
v $2(x + 3) + 3(x + 1) = 39$	**w** $4(x + 3) + 2(3 - x) = 20$	**x** $5x - 2(x + 3) = 3$

5 Solve each of the following equations.

a $3x - 2 = x + 10$	**b** $5y + 1 = 3y + 17$	**c** $8m - 9 = 4m + 11$
d $6e + 5 = 3e + 17$	**e** $7t - 3 = 6t + 7$	**f** $12d - 7 = 5 + 8d$
g $7f + 4 = 12 + 3f$	**h** $2w + 4 = 3w + 2$	**i** $3t + 10 = 5t + 2$
j $2y + 11 = 5y + 2$	**k** $3c + 2 = 8c - 18$	**l** $6x - 3 = 8x - 9$
m $2h + 1 = h - 6$	**n** $3y + 2 = y - 10$	**o** $3a - 6 = 8a + 4$
p $2x + 1 = 7 - x$	**q** $5y + 2 = 10 - 3y$	**r** $c - 4 = 8 - 2c$
s $6d - 5 = 13 - 3d$	**t** $3x - 7 = 3 + 2x$	**u** $7t + 12 = 3 - 2t$
v $5y + 7 = 15 + y$	**w** $3b + 15 = 11 + b$	**x** $6g - 3 = 1 - 7g$

6 Solve each of the following equations.

a $5(x - 2) = 3x$	**b** $2(x + 5) = x + 12$	**c** $3(y - 1) = y + 17$
d $5(d + 4) = 2(d + 13)$	**e** $4(h - 2) = 2(h + 6)$	**f** $10(w - 1) = 4(w + 2)$
g $5(3x - 2) = 4(2x + 1)$	**h** $2(4t - 3) = 3(t + 3)$	**i** $6(d - 2) = 2(2d - 5)$
j $4(3c - 2) = 5(2c - 1)$	**k** $3(2m + 3) = 7(m - 3)$	**l** $4(5y - 2) = 7(3y + 2)$
m $7(m + 3) = 3(2m - 3)$	**n** $5(2y + 3) - 6y = 20$	**o** $2(3t - 5) + 4t = 30$
p $4(2p - 3) = 5p$	**q** $2(2g + 7) - g = 17$	**r** $3(5x - 7) = 8x$
s $3(x - 2) = -5$	**t** $5(x + 5) = 2(x + 7)$	**u** $3(4x + 5) = 7x + 8$
v $3(2 - x) = 3$	**w** $5(4 - 2x) = 10$	**x** $5(6 - 2x) = 2(x + 6)$

7 Decide if each of the following is **always true** or **sometimes true** or **never true**.

a $x + 5 = 5 + x$

b $2x + 3 = 9$

c $3(x + 4) = 3x + 8$

d $5x - 1 = 4$

e $x + 8 = x + 2$

f $6 - x = x - 6$

g $2(x - 4) = 2x - 8$

h $\dfrac{x}{2} = \dfrac{2}{x}$

Exercise B

1 Write an equation for each of the following and solve it to find x.

a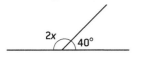

b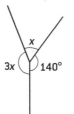

c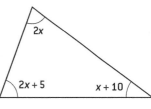

d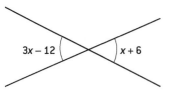

e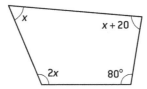

f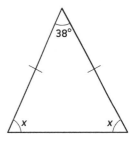

2 Alistair thinks of a number x and multiplies it by 4. He then adds 8. The answer is 56. Form an equation and solve it to find the value of x.

3 Christopher buys three books costing £x each. He also buys two pens costing £1.60 each. His total bill is £15.20. Form an equation and solve it to find the value of x.

4 Sandra buys a drink at x pence. She also buys an apple which costs 10 pence less than the drink. The total cost is £1.30. Form an equation and solve it to find the cost of a drink.

5 A farmer has three fields. The area of the first field is x acres. The area of the second field is twice the area of the first field. The area of the third field is 3 acres less than the area of the second field. The farmer has 27 acres in total. Form an equation in x and solve it to find the area of the biggest field.

6 Shane weighs x kg. Kyle weighs 8 kg more than Shane. Ian weighs 2 kg less than Shane. The total mass of the three boys is 201 kg. Form an equation in x and solve it. Write down Kyle's mass.

Exercise C

1 Use the method of trial and improvement to find a solution for each of the following equations correct to **one decimal place**. You must show all your working.

a $x^2 + 3x = 20$
b $x^2 - 2x = 18$
c $x^3 + x = 84$
d $3x^2 + 5x = 19$
e $4x^2 - 3x = 21$

2 Use the method of trial and improvement to find a solution for each of the following equations correct to **two decimal places**. You must show all your working.

a $x^2 + x = 32$
b $x^2 - x = 15$
c $x^2 + 2x = 112$
d $x^3 + x = 110$
e $2x^2 - 3x = 48$

> **This chapter is about**
> ■ understanding what is meant by similarity
> ■ proving that two triangles are similar.

1 Shapes A and B are given below. In each case decide if A and B are similar or not similar. You must explain your answer.

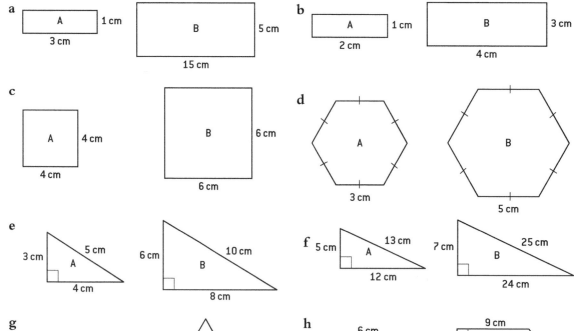

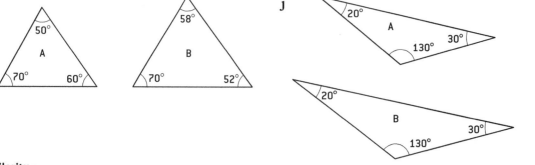

2 Triangles C and D are similar. Find x.

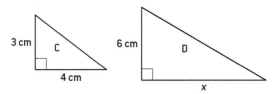

3 Rectangles E and F are similar. Find y.

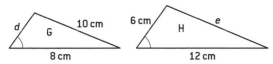

4 Triangles G and H are similar. Find d and e.

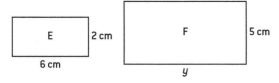

5 Kites I and J are similar. Find x.

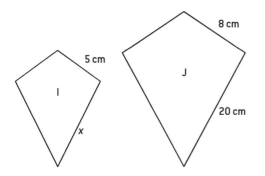

6 Find m.

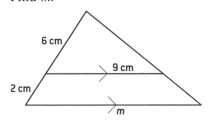

7 Decide whether each statement is **true** or **false**.
  a Two squares are always similar.
  b Two rectangles are always similar.
  c Two circles are always similar.
  d Two parallelograms are always similar.
  e Two regular decagons are always similar.
  f Two kites are always similar.

8 For each pair of parallelograms decide if A and B are similar or not similar. You must explain your answer.
  a

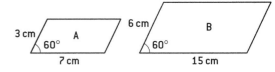

  b

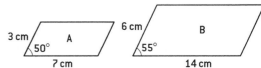

  c

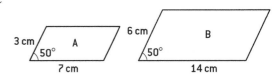

This chapter is about

- using formulae with words and letters
- using negative numbers in formulae
- rearranging a formula
- recognising a formula, an equation, an expression.

Exercise A

1   The cost of an ice-cream is £1.20. A formula for working out the cost of ice-creams is:

cost = £1.20 × number of ice-creams

  a   Use this formula to calculate the cost of
      i 2 ice-creams   **ii** 5 ice-creams   **iii** 10 ice-creams   **iv** 7 ice-creams.
  b   Jason paid £13.20 for ice-creams. How many did he buy?

2   The cost of hiring a jet ski is worked out using the following formula:

hire cost = £15 + (£30 × number of hours hired)

  a   Using the formula calculate the cost of hiring the jet ski for
      i 3 hours   **ii** 8 hours   **iii** $2\frac{1}{2}$ hours.
  b   A family hire the jet ski and pay £195 in total. How long did they hire the jet ski for?

3   A plumber uses the following formula when charging customers to service appliances:

cost = call out fee + (£20 × number of hours)

  Given that the call out fee is £30, work out what the plumber charges for:
  a   an oil boiler that took 2 hours to service
  b   a gas boiler that took half an hour to service
  c   an oil cooker that took an hour and a half to service
  d   a gas fire that took 1 hour 45 minutes to service.

4   A waitress is paid £5.60 per hour plus a weekly bonus of £25.
    Calculate how much she earns each week when:
    a   she works 32 hours   b   she works 41 hours   c   she works 27.5 hours.

5   The time taken to cook roast beef is given by the formula:

time taken (in minutes) = 30 minutes + (weight in pounds × 45 minutes)

  a   Use the formula to calculate the time taken to cook a roast that weighs
      i 3 pounds   **ii** 8 pounds   **iii** 5 pounds   **iv** $4\frac{1}{2}$ pounds.
  b   Marie cooked her roast for 3 hours and 30 minutes. Calculate the weight of her roast.

6   A pen costs 75 pence. Write a formula for the cost C (in pence) of x pens.

7   A book costs £3.50. Write a formula for the cost C (in £) of y books.

8   An apple costs 25p and a pear costs 30p. Write a formula for the total cost C (in pence) of x apples and y pears.

9   A van has four wheels and a lorry has six wheels. Write down a formula for the total number of wheels W on m vans and n lorries.

10 Zoe gets paid £6.80 per hour plus £0.40 per mile for mileage.

  a Write down a formula for the total pay P (in £) that Zoe receives when she works H hours and travels M miles.

  b Use your formula to calculate how much Zoe would receive on a day when she
  i works 8 hours and travels 22 miles   **ii** works 6 hours and does no mileage.

  c One week in March she received £286. Given that she travelled 120 miles that week, work out how many hours she worked.

Exercise B

1 Given that $T = 2m + 3n$, find T when $m = 3$ and $n = 2$.

2 Given that $W = x^2 - y$, find W when $x = 4$ and $y = 3$.

3 Given that $D = 5c - 2e$, find D when $c = 8$ and $e = 3$.

4 Given that $H = 3(2d - g)$, find H when $d = 5$ and $g = 2$.

5 Given that $L = 3y^2 + 5y$, find L when $y = 2$.

6 Given that $A = \dfrac{4ew + e}{w}$, find A when $e = 6$ and $w = 2$.

7 Given that $C = \dfrac{7y(x - 2y)}{3}$, find C when $y = 3$ and $x = 10$.

8 Given that $B = 4Y + 3X$, find Y when $B = 18$ and $X = 2$.

9 Given that $M = 2E - 5T$, find E when $M = 5$ and $T = 3$.

10 Given that $T = 2(y + x)$, find y when $T = 22$ and $x = 7$.

11 Given that $A = 3c + 2d$, find A when $c = 5$ and $d = -3$.

12 Given that $T = 5x + 4y$, find T when $x = 4$ and $y = -2$.

13 Given that $C = 7e + 6d$, find C when $e = -2$ and $d = -1$.

14 Given that $W = 3m - 2n$, find W when $m = -3$ and $n = -5$.

15 Given that $B = g^2 + 3h$, find B when $g = -5$ and $h = -4$.

16 Given that $F = c(d + 2p)$, find F when $c = -4$, $d = 8$ and $p = -3$.

17 Given that $M = \dfrac{n(p - n)}{p}$, find M when $n = 8$ and $p = -2$.

18 Given that $L = R(A + 2B)$, find A when $L = 6$, $B = 4$ and $R = 3$.

19 Given that $D = 3Q(R - N)$, find N when $D = 30$, $R = -6$ and $Q = -5$.

20 Given that $X = \dfrac{2C(3 - M)}{5}$, find C when $X = 8$ and $M = -2$.

21 Decide if each of the following is an **expression** or an **equation** or a **formula**.

  a $4x + 1 = 9$ **b** $3x + 2$

  c $F = ma$ **d** $4y - 2x$

  e $2x - 1 = x + 5$ **f** $v = u + at$

  g $4(x - 2) = 3$ **h** $A = bh$

  i $3y + 4x - z$ **j** $C = \pi d$

  k $8 - 5m$ **l** $7 - y = 3y - 1$

22 Given that **n is a positive integer** write down whether each of the following is always odd, always even or could be odd or even.
You must give a reason for your answer.

a	$2n$	**b**	$5n$	**c**	$2n + 1$	**d**	$4n + 6$
e	$3n + 2$	**f**	$2n + 4$	**g**	$6n - 1$	**h**	$5n + 2$

Exercise C

1 In each case make x the subject of the formula.

a $x + 4 = y$ **b** $x + t = w$ **c** $x - 4 = 12y$ **d** $x - 2p = m$

e $3 + x = 2y$ **f** $9c + x = 2t$ **g** $3x = q$ **h** $7x = 4m$

i $4x = 3y$ **j** $wx = y$ **k** $xy = z$ **l** $tx = 3w$

m $\dfrac{x}{4} = w$ **n** $\dfrac{x}{p} = q$ **o** $\dfrac{x}{3} = wm$ **p** $\dfrac{x}{3w} = 2t$

q $x + 7c = 2d$ **r** $8x = 11g$ **s** $8h + x = 7k$ **t** $abx = ef$

2 In each case make x the subject of the formula.

a $gh = x$ **b** $3 + h = x$ **c** $c - h = x$ **d** $\dfrac{w}{h} = x$

e $w = x + 5$ **f** $hg = x - d$ **g** $p = 3x$ **h** $cd = \dfrac{x}{7}$

i $ef = x - c$ **j** $jk = x + t$ **k** $fg = kx$ **l** $8y = \dfrac{x}{m}$

m $kp = x + t + d$ **n** $w + k = 2ax$ **o** $a - 2b = 3w + x$ **p** $dm = 3xy$

3 In each case make x the subject of the formula.

a $2x + y = w$ **b** $2x + 1 = m$ **c** $3x - 2 = t$ **d** $4x + 5 = e$

e $10x - 4 = n$ **f** $2x + y = c$ **g** $4x - d = m$ **h** $6x + k = w$

i $5x - g = 2t$ **j** $3x + e = 5e$ **k** $2x - m = 12m$ **l** $7x + 2n = 3n$

m $4x - 3y = 2y$ **n** $nx + t = g$ **o** $ex - y^2 = m$ **p** $\dfrac{x + d}{4} = e$

q $\dfrac{x - c}{5} = d$ **r** $\dfrac{2x - y}{3} = h$ **s** $\dfrac{kx + n}{4} = I$ **t** $\dfrac{x}{2} + 3 = m$

u $\dfrac{x}{3} - n = e$ **v** $\dfrac{x}{5} + t = c$ **w** $\dfrac{x}{w} - 5 = d$ **x** $\dfrac{x}{gh} + y = D$

4 In each case make x the subject of the formula.

a $y = 3 - x$ **b** $y = c - x$ **c** $3p = 8 - x$ **d** $gh = t - x$

e $5 - x = t$ **f** $n - x = 4$ **g** $5y - x = w$ **h** $10w - x = w$

i $d = 3 - x$ **j** $y = m^2 - x$ **k** $m - 2x = t$ **l** $e - 4x = d$

m $k = L - 3x$ **n** $4y = y - 5x$ **o** $3 = m - \dfrac{x}{4}$ **p** $C = d - \dfrac{x}{5}$

q $g = \dfrac{h - x}{4}$ **r** $I = \dfrac{n - x}{c}$ **s** $ed = \dfrac{3 - 2x}{5}$ **t** $y = \dfrac{h - gx}{t}$

5 In each case make x the subject of the formula.

a $3(x + n) = e$ **b** $5(x - 2) = c$ **c** $4(3 + x) = d$ **d** $7(3j + x) = m$

e $h(x + 2) = i$ **f** $m(x - 3) = t$ **g** $3(n - x) = y$ **h** $5(2 - x) = g$

i $w = 4(t - x)$ **j** $f = i(3 - x)$ **k** $L = k(m - x)$ **l** $m = 3(2x - t)$

m $w(y - x) = 3d$ **n** $5t = 3(f - x)$ **o** $2 = 3(p - x)$ **p** $3d = 2(y - x)$

CHAPTER 42

Midpoint and length of line segments

This chapter is about

- finding the midpoint of a line joining two points
- finding the length of a line joining two points.

1 Find the co-ordinates of the midpoint of the line segment whose end points are

a (1, 2) and (3, 6)	**b** (4, 4) and (6, 8)	**c** (3, 7) and (1, 9)
d (4, 5) and (0, 9)	**e** (4, 7) and (10, 8)	**f** (−3, 5) and (5, −1)
g (2, 1) and (−6, 5)	**h** (−3, −5) and (1, 3)	**i** (−8, 2) and (−4, −2)
j (5, 9) and (6, −2)	**k** (11, −8) and (−7, 3)	**l** (9, 0) and (−4, −5)

2 In the following you are given the co-ordinates of the midpoint of each line segment, and the co-ordinates of one of the end points. Find the co-ordinates of the other end point.

a Midpoint of AB is (3, 4). A has co-ordinates (4, 6). Find the co-ordinates of B.

b Midpoint of CD is (2, 1). C has co-ordinates (3, 2). Find the co-ordinates of D.

c Midpoint of EF is (5, 3). F has co-ordinates (7, 7). Find the co-ordinates of E.

d Midpoint of GH is (2, 0). H has co-ordinates (1, 1). Find the co-ordinates of G.

e Midpoint of IJ is (−1, 1). I has co-ordinates (−3, −2). Find the co-ordinates of J.

f Midpoint of KL is $(\frac{1}{2}, 3)$. L has co-ordinates (1, 0). Find the co-ordinates of K.

g Midpoint of MN is (−3, −2). N has co-ordinates (−7, 0). Find the co-ordinates of M.

h Midpoint of PQ is $(-1\frac{1}{2}, -3\frac{1}{2})$. P has co-ordinates (−2, −1). Find the co-ordinates of Q.

3 Find the length of the line segment joining each pair of co-ordinates. If necessary give your answer to 2 decimal places.

a (0, 0) and (6, 8)	**b** (2, 1) and (5, 5)	**c** (3, 0) and (8, 12)
d (4, 10) and (2, 1)	**e** (−3, 7) and (4, 11)	**f** (2, −4) and (−1, 5)
g (−3, 8) and (−8, 2)	**h** (1, 9) and (−7, −1)	**i** (4, −3) and (−9, 10)
j (0, −4) and (6, 0)	**k** (−3, 12) and (−8, −2)	**l** (−7, −5) and (−1, 0)

4 A has co-ordinates (−3, 7) and B has co-ordinates (4, 4). Find

a the midpoint of the line segment AB

b the length of the line segment AB, giving your answer to three decimal places.

5 P has co-ordinates (5, −3) and Q has co-ordinates (9, 2). Find

a the midpoint of the line segment PQ

b the length of the line segment PQ, giving your answer to one decimal place.

6 L, M and N lie in a straight line, where M is the midpoint of LN. L has co-ordinates (1, 3) and M has co-ordinates (5, 5). Find the length of the line segment LN. Give your answer to two decimal places.

CHAPTER 43

Metric and imperial units

This chapter is about

- recognising metric and imperial units
- knowing how to convert between certain metric and imperial units.

1 Write down the **metric** units of length from the following list.
   miles, grams, metres, litres, centimetres, feet

2 Write down the **imperial** units of length from the following list.
   yards, kilograms, pints, inches, kilometres, pounds

3 Write down the **metric** units of mass from the following list.
   ounces, feet, grams, litres, tonnes, miles

4 Write down the **imperial** units of mass from the following list.
   kilograms, stones, miles, pounds, metres, gallons

5 Write down the **metric** units of capacity from the following list.
   litres, grams, millilitres, pints, millimetres, gallons

6 Write down the **imperial** units of capacity from the following list.
   pounds, pints, metres, gallons, inches, yards

7

| millimetres | grams | litres | metres | kilograms |
| milligrams | centimetres | millilitres | kilometres | |

From the list of **metric** units, select an appropriate unit to measure:

a the length of a bungalow   b the mass of a television
c the capacity of a bottle of shampoo   d the mass of a grape
e the height of a bumble bee   f the capacity of a large bucket

8

| pounds | feet | gallons | yards | ounces |
| stones | inches | pints | miles | |

From the list of **imperial** units, select an appropriate unit to measure:

a the distance from Omagh to Armagh   b the mass of a roast beef
c the volume of water in a swimming pool   d the length of a supermarket
e the capacity of an oil drum   f the mass of a large dog

9 Work out the following approximate conversions.
   a 6 kg to lb   b 2.5 kg to lb   c 22 lb to kg
   d 8 lb to kg   e 20 miles to km   f 12 miles to km
   g 64 km to miles   h 100 km to miles   i 16 litres to pints
   j 3 litres to pints k 14 pints to litres l 30 pints to litres
   m 66 lb to kg   n 70 miles to km   o 6 litres to pints
   p 19 kg to lb   q 3 miles to metres   r $\frac{1}{2}$ mile to metres

10 Given that 1 gallon is approximately 4.5 litres, calculate how many litres are equivalent to 6 gallons.

11 Given that 1 inch is approximately 2.5 cm, work out the length in cm of a 4 inch nail.

12 A recipe book gives the approximation 1 oz = 25 g. Work out how many ounces of flour are needed in a recipe which says to use 60 g of flour.

13 The distance from Belfast to Dublin is 100 miles. What is the distance in km?

14 Ted bought five 2-litre cartons of milk last week. How many pints did he buy?

15 Henry travels at 40 mph. What speed is this in km/h?

16 The distance from Laura's home to her place of work is 9.5 miles. Work out the total distance she travels to and from work over a 5-day week. Give your answer in km.

17 A chocolate cake contains 12 oz of sugar. How many grams of sugar are there in the chocolate cake?

CHAPTER 44

Sequences 3

This chapter is about

- generating sequences and finding rules for generating a given sequence
- finding and using the nth term of an arithmetic sequence.

1 Write down the rule and the next two terms for each of the following sequences.

  a 3, 8, 13, 18, ___, ___   **b** 4, 8, 16, 32, ___, ___

  c 40, 37, 34, 31, ___, ___   **d** 10, 16, 22, 28, ___, ___

  e 0.7, 7, 70, 700, ___, ___   **f** 22, 17, 12, 7, ___, ___

  g 6, 6.4, 6.8, 7.2, ___, ___   **h** 96, 48, 24, 12, ___, ___

2 Work out the first five terms of each sequence when the nth term is given as

  a $3n$ **b** $2n + 1$ **c** $4n - 2$

  d $5n - 1$ **e** $-2n$ **f** $-3n + 1$

  g $6 - n$ **h** $20 - 3n$ **i** n^2

  j $n^2 + 3$ **k** n^3 **l** $\dfrac{60}{n}$

  m $\dfrac{n}{2}$ **n** $\dfrac{n}{n + 1}$ **o** $\dfrac{n^2}{n^3}$

3 For each sequence whose nth term is given below, work out

  i the 10th term   **ii** the 50th term.

  a $2n$ **b** $3n - 10$ **c** $4n + 1$

  d $20 - n$ **e** $-3n$ **f** $-2n + 15$

  g n^2 **h** $\dfrac{n}{100}$ **i** $\dfrac{100}{n}$

4 Work out the nth term for each of the following sequences.

  a 5, 10, 15, 20, …   **b** 5, 7, 9, 11, …

  c 5, 9, 13, 17, …   **d** 2, 5, 8, 11, …

  e 3, 8, 13, 18, …   **f** 13, 23, 33, 43, …

  g 6, 7, 8, 9, …   **h** 8, 14, 20, 26, …

  i 1, 5, 9, 13, …   **j** 7, 9, 11, 13, …

  k −3, −6, −9, −12, …   **l** −10, −20, −30, −40, …

  m 8, 6, 4, 2, …   **n** 6, 3, 0, −3, …

  o −3, −8, −13, −18, …   **p** −3, −5, −7, −9, …

  q 5, 4, 3, 2, …   **r** −7, −6, −5, −4, …

5 This is a sequence of squares made from matchsticks.

  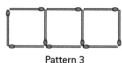

Pattern 1   Pattern 2   Pattern 3

  a Draw the next two patterns.

  b Copy and complete this table showing the number of matchsticks used.

Pattern number	1	2	3	4	5
Number of matchsticks	4				

c How many matchsticks are used to make pattern 10?
d Which pattern number has 49 matchsticks?
e Rhonda says she can make one of the patterns using 80 matchsticks. Is she correct? Explain your answer.

6 This is a sequence of squares made from black and white tiles.

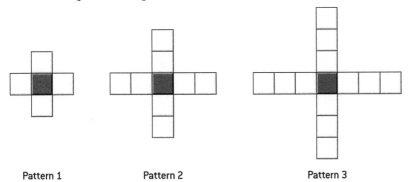

Pattern 1   Pattern 2   Pattern 3

a Draw the next pattern.
b Copy and complete this table showing the number of tiles used.

Pattern number	1	2	3	4
Number of black tiles				
Number of white tiles				
Total number of tiles				

c Find a rule in terms of n to work out
 i the number of white tiles
 ii the total number of black and white tiles.
d Which pattern number has 44 white tiles?
e Which pattern number has 53 tiles altogether?
f Dougie's pattern has 97 tiles is total. Which pattern number is it?

7 This is a sequence made up of tables and chairs.

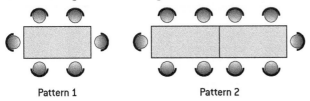

Pattern 1   Pattern 2

a Draw the next pattern.
b Copy and complete this table showing the number of tables and chairs.

Pattern number	1	2	3	4
Number of tables				
Number of chairs				

c Find a rule to work out the number of chairs needed for any given number of tables.
d Which pattern number has 30 chairs?
e How many tables are needed when there are 50 chairs?

CHAPTER 45 Approximating and estimating 2

This chapter is about

- using estimation within calculations involving whole numbers and decimals
- having several strategies for checking answers
- multiplying and dividing by numbers between 0 and 1
- finding reciprocals.

Exercise A

1 **Estimate** the answer to each of the following. Show all your working.

a $39 + 54$	**b** $684 - 251$	**c** 28×65
d $63 \div 29$	**e** $28.5 + 7.4$	**f** 3.14×9.46
g $8.6 + 11.9 + 0.23$	**h** 0.67×0.22	**i** 3.77^2
j $819 \div 24$	**k** 644×581	**l** $732 + 57.4 + 6.28$
m $0.94 - 0.18$	**n** $1022 + 38.2 + 0.77$	**o** 84×113
p $24 + 369 - 17.2$	**q** 0.81^2	**r** $234 + 387 - 33.8$
s 12.3×58.44	**t** $224 - 36.99$	**u** 37.9^2
v $1988 + 17.4 + 0.4$	**w** $808 \div 23.1$	**x** 31.4×3.2^2

2 **Estimate** the answer to each calculation. Show all your working.

a $\dfrac{6.8 \times 18.4}{1.7}$ **b** $\dfrac{59.5 + 86.4}{5.21}$ **c** $\dfrac{13.4 + 42.9}{8.9 - 4.4}$

d $\dfrac{294 - 115}{9.12 - 5.03}$ **e** $\dfrac{67.3 \times 28.4}{1.65 + 0.97}$ **f** $\dfrac{38.55 \times 63.04}{91.7 - 13.74}$

g $\dfrac{38 + 36}{0.21}$ **h** $\dfrac{81.4 - 22.3}{0.43 - 0.14}$ **i** $\dfrac{5.8 \times 2.4^2}{0.63 - 0.49}$

j $\dfrac{23.7 \times 52.06}{\sqrt{3.77}}$ **k** $\dfrac{1.8^2 \times 3.41^2}{5.85}$ **l** $\dfrac{215 + 555}{\sqrt{118}}$

3 There were 4851 supporters at a football match. Each ticket for the match cost £12. Estimate the total amount of money paid for tickets.

4 On average each cow on Matt's farm produces 32.7 litres of milk every day. He has 78 cows. Estimate the amount of milk produced per day on the farm.

5 A shipping container contains 780 boxes. Each box contains 120 light-bulbs. Estimate the total number of light-bulbs in the container.

6 There are 665 pupils at Park High School. The school gives £2.15 per child towards raising money for a new minibus out of the school fund. Estimate how much money is given.

7 Estimate how many boxes of cornflakes, costing £1.89 each, Mrs Green can buy with £10.

8 Estimate the 'miles per gallon' for a car that can cover 635 miles on 11.2 gallons of diesel.

9 Estimate the total cost of a holiday when the flights cost £319, accommodation costs were £289 and the total spending money was £780.

10 A packet of cigarettes costs £7.85. For a smoker who consumes one packet each day, estimate how much he will spend:
a each week   **b** in the month of May   **c** in a year.

11 Jordan is travelling from London to Johannesburg. The total journey is 5309 miles. Two hours into the flight he has travelled 622 miles. Estimate the number of miles remaining.

12 A rectangular field is 182.5 m by 243 m. Estimate:
a its area   **b** its perimeter.

13 Estimate the value of each square root, giving your answer to one decimal place.

a $\sqrt{26}$ **b** $\sqrt{48}$ **c** $\sqrt{30}$ **d** $\sqrt{105}$ **e** $\sqrt{18}$

f $\sqrt{155}$ **g** $\sqrt{54}$ **h** $\sqrt{125}$ **i** $\sqrt{77}$ **j** $\sqrt{200}$

Exercise B

1 For each calculation, write down another calculation you could use to check if the answer is correct.
a $56 + 93 = 149$ **b** $283 - 97 = 186$ **c** $65 \times 23 = 1495$
d $1600 \div 25 = 64$ **e** $9.8 \times 6.35 = 62.23$ **f** $28.5^2 = 812.25$

g $\dfrac{2394}{28.5} = 84$

2 Given that $12 \times 860 = 10\,320$, write down the answer to:
a 120×86
b $10\,320 \div 86$
c 1.2×8.6
d $1032 \div 1.2$

3 Given that $14.25 \times 280 = 3990$, write down the answer to:
a 142.5×2.8
b $3990 \div 28$
c $399 \div 14.25$
d 1.425×2.8

4 Given that $\dfrac{2025}{60} = 33.75$, write down the answer to:
a $\dfrac{20.25}{6}$
b 6000×33.75
c 0.6×3.375
d $\dfrac{20\,250}{33.75}$

5 Work out the following.
   a 0.8 × 0.4   b 0.6 × 0.3   c 0.6 × 0.5   d 0.2 × 0.3
   e 0.4 × 0.1   f 0.2 × 12   g 0.3 × 21   h 0.6 × 11
   i 0.5 × 23   j 0.7 × 13   k 0.9 × 62   l 0.4 × 120
   m 0.8 × 36   n 0.6 × 58   o 0.3 × 147   p 0.4 × 216

6 Work out the following.
   a 12 ÷ 0.2   b 20 ÷ 0.4   c 17 ÷ 0.1   d 72 ÷ 0.8
   e 8 ÷ 0.02   f 15 ÷ 0.03   g 1.8 ÷ 0.3   h 12.5 ÷ 0.05
   i 324 ÷ 0.6   j 116 ÷ 0.8   k 145.6 ÷ 0.04 l 33.74 ÷ 0.07
   m 56.28 ÷ 0.3   n 9.45 ÷ 0.9   o 0.217 ÷ 0.02 p 1.79 ÷ 0.05

7 Siobhan says that when you multiply a number by 5 the answer is always bigger than 5. Is she correct? Explain your answer.

8 There are 100 paper clips, to the nearest 10, in a box.
   a What is the minimum number of paper clips in the box?
   b What is the maximum number of paper clips in the box?
   c What is the minimum number of paper clips in 5 boxes?
   d What is the maximum number of paper clips in 6 boxes?

9 There are 800 people, to the nearest 100, at a concert.
   a What is the minimum number of people at the concert?
   b What is the maximum number of people at the concert?

10 Una's height is 96 cm to the nearest cm. What are the minimum and maximum values for Una's height?

11 An office measures 8 m by 5 m, both to the nearest metre. What are the minimum and maximum measurements of the office?

12 Write down the reciprocal of each of the following.

   a $\dfrac{2}{3}$ b $\dfrac{1}{5}$ c 8   d 10

   e $\dfrac{4}{5}$ f $1\dfrac{1}{3}$ g $2\dfrac{1}{4}$ h $4\dfrac{2}{3}$

   i 0.4   j 1.4   k 5.75   l 3.01

13 What number does not have a reciprocal?

14 What is the missing number in each of the following?

   a $6 \times \square = 1$ b $\dfrac{3}{8} \times \square = 1$

   c $1.2 \times \square = 1$ d $4\dfrac{1}{10} \times \square = 1$

   e $3.35 \times \square = 1$ f $-\dfrac{1}{5} \times \square = 1$

CHAPTER 46

The order of operations and index laws in algebra

This chapter is about

- applying operations in the correct order (BODMAS)
- applying the index laws to algebraic expressions.

Exercise A

1 Work out the following.

a	$5 + 4 \times 2$	**b**	$10 + 8 \div 2$	**c**	$6 \times 2 - 1$
d	$15 - 4 \times 3$	**e**	$7 \times 2 + 1$	**f**	$10 - 6 + 2$
g	$6 + 3 \times 3$	**h**	$20 - 5 \times 2$	**i**	$20 + 15 \div 5$
j	$30 - 20 \div 2$	**k**	$20 \div 2 + 2$	**l**	$15 - 8 + 3$
m	$16 - 3 - 2$	**n**	$7 \times 8 - 4$	**o**	$50 - 20 \div 10$
p	$7 + 24 \div 4$	**q**	$12 - 8 \div 4$	**r**	$3 + 15 \div 3$
s	$18 - 3 \times 6$	**t**	$40 + 30 \div 5$	**u**	$12 - 6 + 2$
v	$20 \times 4 \div 2$	**w**	$60 \div 10 \times 5$	**x**	$12 - 8 \div 2 + 6$

2 Work out the following.

a	$3 \times (2 + 4)$	**b**	$(8 + 10) \div 2$	**c**	$12 - (3 + 3)$
d	$15 \div (2 + 1)$	**e**	$10 \times (7 - 4)$	**f**	$(3 + 4) \times 5$
g	$12 - (7 - 2)$	**h**	$(3 + 2) \times (6 - 2)$	**i**	$(5 - 4) \times (3 + 4)$
j	$(6 + 8) \div (7 - 5)$	**k**	$3 \times 8 \div (8 - 2)$	**l**	$30 \div 5 \times (7 - 4)$
m	$16 - (8 - 6)$	**n**	$(12 - 6 - 4) \times (1 + 5 - 3)$	**o**	$(2 - 5) \times 4$
p	$(-8 - 2) \div 2$	**q**	$(-3 - 4) \times (5 - 2)$	**r**	$20 - 12 \div (7 - 3)$
s	$8 + (3 \times 4 - 3)$	**t**	$4 \times (9 \div 3 + 5)$	**u**	$(20 \div 4) \times 3 - 4$
v	$(-4 - 6) \div (1 - 3)$	**w**	$18 - (3 \times 4) \div 3$	**x**	$((5 + 3) \times 2) \times 7$

3 Work out the following.

a	5^2	**b**	4^3	**c**	$6^2 + 10$
d	$7^2 - 5$	**e**	$3^2 \times 6$	**f**	2×4^2
g	$5^2 + 2^3$	**h**	$3^3 - 2^2$	**i**	$(6 + 4)^2$
j	$(10 - 2)^2$	**k**	$(7 + 2)^2 \times 2$	**l**	$(5 - 1)^3 \div 2$
m	$5 \times (6^2 - 4^2)$	**n**	$(3 - 1)^4 \times 3$	**o**	$(3^2 - 2^2)^2$
p	$5^2 - (5 \times 2^2)$	**q**	$(5 - 3)^2 \times (12 \div 4)^2$	**r**	$7^2 - 3^2 \times 2$
s	$(18 \div 6)^2 - 2^2$	**t**	$(3^2 + 4^2) \times 3$	**u**	$(10^2 - 8^2) \times 3^2$
v	$(7 - 3)^2 - (4 \div 2)^2$	**w**	$3^2 - (10 - 6)^2$	**x**	$(3 - 7)^2$

4 Work out the following.

a	$5 \times 3 + 6 \times 2$	**b**	$3 \times 4 + 8 \div 2$	**c**	$7 \times 4 - 2 \times 4$
d	$20 \div 4 + 1 \times 3$	**e**	$12 \div 2 + 2 \div 2$	**f**	$3 \times 6 - 2 \times 3$
g	$5 + 3^2 \times 2$	**h**	$20 - 4^2 \div 2$	**i**	$18 \div 3^2 + 1$

j $5 + (12 - 4) \div 2$ **k** $30 - (2 + 1)^2 + 6$ **l** $(16 - 7) \times (8 - 3)^2$
m $24 - (12 - 3) \div 3$ **n** $50 - 5 \times 4 + 2$ **o** $60 + 10 \div 2 + 8 \times 3^2$
p $3 + 5 \times (3^2 - 4)$ **q** $40 - 24 \div (4^2 \div 2)$ **r** $36 \div 3^2 - 7$
s $15 \div 5 - 3^2 \times 2$ **t** $19 + (2 + 3)^2 - 11$ **u** $20 + 30 \div 5 - 3$
v $(3^2 + 6^2) \div 5 + 4$ **w** $11 \times (3^2 - 4^2)$ **x** $3 \times 4 + 8 \div 2^2 - 14$

5 Copy these statements and insert brackets to make them correct.
  a $8 \times 7 - 4 = 24$ **b** $20 \div 2 + 3 = 4$
  c $3 + 4 \times 2 = 14$ **d** $10 - 4 \times 3 = 18$
  e $10 - 3 + 7 = 0$ **f** $6 \times 1 + 4 = 30$
  g $2 + 3 \times 6 - 1 = 25$ **h** $3 \times 2 + 1 \times 2 = 18$
  i $6 + 8 \times 7 - 4 = 30$ **j** $12 + 6 \div 5 - 2 = 6$
  k $11 - 4 \times 3 + 2 = 35$ **l** $6 - 2^2 \times 3 = 48$

6 Find the missing number in each of the following.
  a $3 + 5 \times \square = 13$ **b** $12 - 6 \div \square = 10$
  c $\square + 4 \times 3 = 18$ **d** $\square - 3 \times 3 = 12$
  e $\square \times 6 + 2 = 26$ **f** $3 + \square \times 8 = 35$
  g $30 - \square \div 2 = 18$ **h** $(\square + 5)^2 \times 2 = 72$
  i $5 \times (\square - 3)^2 = 80$ **j** $3 \times (7 - \square)^3 = 81$
  k $(3^2 - 5) \times 2^\square = 32$ **l** $(8 - 4)^\square - 11 = 53$

Exercise B

1 Write each of the following expressions as a single power.
  a $x^4 \times x^2$ **b** $x^{10} \times x^4$ **c** $x \times x^5$
  d $w^3 \times w^{10}$ **e** $k^8 \times k^8$ **f** $h^{11} \times h^{12}$

2 Write each of the following expressions as a single power.
  a $y^8 \div y^2$ **b** $y^{12} \div y^3$ **c** $y^7 \div y^2$
  d $g^{13} \div g^6$ **e** $x^{10} \div x$ **f** $x^3 \div x^6$

3 Write each of the following expressions as a single power.
  a $(y^4)^3$ **b** $(y^2)^7$ **c** $(y^5)^5$
  d $(x^3)^6$ **e** $(m^5)^{11}$ **f** $(t^5)^0$

4 Write each of the following expressions as a single power.
  a $x^{14} \times x^2$ **b** $y^5 \div y^8$ **c** $y^4 \times y^2 \times y$
  d $(n^8)^7$ **e** $x^2 \times x^6 \times x$ **f** $(y^7)^1$
  g $(m^5 \div m^3)^3$ **h** $\dfrac{m^4 \times m^6}{m^2}$ **i** $\dfrac{m \times m^4}{m^7}$
  j $\dfrac{m^9 \times m^3}{m^2 \times m^2}$ **k** $\dfrac{m^7 \times m^8}{m \times m^5}$ **l** $\dfrac{m^6 \times m^5}{(m^2)^2}$
  m $\dfrac{y^{10} \div y^2}{y^4}$ **n** $\dfrac{(y^5)^4}{y^8 \div y^3}$ **o** $\dfrac{(m^4)^6}{(m^3)^7}$

CHAPTER 47

Money and percentages

> ## This chapter is about
>
> - calculating the credit charge when buying goods on hire purchase
> - understanding and calculating net pay, taking into account income tax and National Insurance contributions
> - using currency exchange rates.

1 A wheelbarrow costs £38 plus VAT at 20%.
   a How much is the VAT?   **b** What is the total cost of the wheelbarrow?

2 A coat has a marked price of £54. In a sale there is 30% off. What is the cost of the coat in the sale?

3 A computer costs £380 cash. It can be bought on hire purchase for a deposit of £50 followed by 24 instalments of £18.
   a What is the cost of buying the computer on hire purchase?
   b What is the difference between the cash price and the hire purchase price?

4 A car costs £13750 cash. It can be bought for a deposit of 20% of the cash price followed by 48 monthly instalments of £259.
   Work out the difference in the cost between buying the car on hire purchase and buying the car outright from the start.

5 Vincent has a part time job which pays £8 per hour. When he works on a Saturday he gets paid time and a half. Calculate Vincent's total pay one week when he worked 3 hours on Thursday, 5 hours on Friday and 6 hours on Saturday.

6 Lily earns £6 per hour in her job. When she works on a bank holiday she gets paid double time. One week her pay was £114. She worked 5 hours on the bank holiday Monday, 3 hours on Friday and the rest of the time on Wednesday. How many hours did she work on Wednesday?

7 Jessica sells jewellery. Each month she receives a basic wage plus 3% commission on all the jewellery that she sells that month.
   Her basic wage for each month is £900. In August she sold £8000 worth of jewellery. What was her total pay for the month of August?

8 Naomi earns £30000 per year. The first £5000 is tax-free. She then pays income tax at a rate of 24%.
   a How much tax does she pay?
   b How much does she have left after tax?

9 Orla earns £68000 per year. The first £8000 is tax-free. She pays income tax at 36%. How much income tax does she pay?

10 Given that £1 = €1.18 convert each of the following.

   a £12 into euros   **b** £300 into euros   **c** £68.50 into euros
   d €236 into pounds   **e** €41.30 into pounds   **f** €62 into pounds
   g Grace went to Paris and converted £200 into euros. Whilst away she spent €138. She returned home and converted the remaining euros into £ at the same exchange rate. Calculate how many £ she received.

11 Given that £1 = US $1.5214 convert each of the following.

  a £1200 into dollars   **b** £450 into dollars   **c** £118 into dollars
  d $7607 into pounds   **e** $68 463 into pounds   **f** $ 540 into pounds
  g Shauna goes to the USA. While she is there she buys jeans costing $35. When she returns home she sees the same jeans for sale costing £60. Using the same exchange rate work out how much Shauna has saved in £ by purchasing the jeans in the USA.

12 Given that £1 = €1.14 and that €1 = $1.27 convert each of the following.

  a £24 into euros   **b** €300 into pounds   **c** €250 into dollars
  d $1248 into euros   **e** £420 into dollars   **f** $1280 into pounds
  g A retired couple would like to buy a painting whilst on holiday in New York. The limit on their Visa account means that they can afford to spend £1500. The painting costs $2000. Work out whether they will have enough money to purchase the painting.

13 Study the electricity bill below.

Previous reading	Present reading	Price per unit (pence)
27 496	28 841	13.08

a Units consumed =   **c** VAT at 5% = £

b Cost of units = £   **d** Total cost = £

  a Work out how many units of electricity were used.
  b Work out the cost of the electricity used.
  c Work out the VAT to be paid.
  d Work out the total cost including the VAT.

14 Below is a bank statement with missing values.

		Credit	Debit	Current balance
14 April				£87.84 dr
15 April	Lodgement	£120		£32.16
21 April	O'Neills Butchers		£13.35	**a** £_____
24 April	Direct debit NIE		£48.00	**b** £_____
28 April	Mortgage payment		£458.35	**c** £_____
30 April	Salary	£1458.34		**d** £_____

Work out the current balance on

  a 21 April   **b** 24 April   **c** 28 April   **d** 30 April.
  e There is an overdraft limit of £1500 on this account. Work out the maximum amount of money that can be withdrawn from this account on 30th April.

This chapter is about
- constructing triangles
- constructing the perpendicular bisector of a straight line
- constructing the bisector of an angle
- constructing a perpendicular from a point to a straight line
- constructing loci.

Exercise A

1 a Construct triangle ABC.
  b Measure the length of BC.

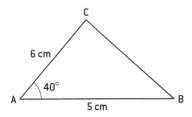

2 a Construct triangle PQR.
  b Measure the length of PR.

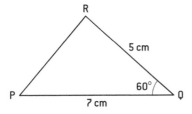

3 a Construct triangle LMN.
  b Measure the length of LN.

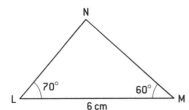

4 a Construct triangle DEF.
  b Measure the length of FE.
  c Measure the length of DF.

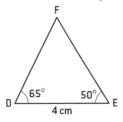

5 a Construct triangle GHI.
  b Measure the angle IGH.

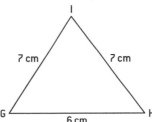

6 a Construct triangle XYZ.
  b Measure the angle XZY.

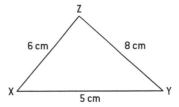

7 a Construct parallelogram ABCD.
b Measure the angle ABC.

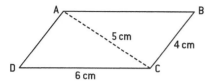

8 a Construct trapezium PQRS.
b Measure the length of QR.

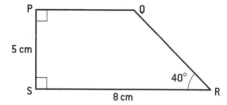

9 a Construct a rhombus with sides of length 5 cm and shorter diagonal of length 4 cm.
b Measure the length of the longer diagonal.

10 a Construct a rhombus with sides of length 6 cm and longer diagonal of length 10 cm.
b Measure the length of the shorter diagonal.

Exercise B

1 Draw a horizontal line 7 cm long and label it AB.
a Construct the perpendicular bisector of the line AB.
b Measure the distance from A to the midpoint of AB.

2 Draw a vertical line 6 cm long. Construct the perpendicular bisector of the line.

3 Draw a horizontal line CD 12 cm long. Mark the point T on the line that is 4 cm from C. Construct a line perpendicular to CD that passes through T.

4 Draw a vertical line PQ 10 cm long. Mark the point R on the line that is 3 cm from P. Construct a line perpendicular to PQ that passes through R.

5 Draw a horizontal line 12 cm long and label it XY. Mark the point P so that it is 4 cm to the right of X and 2 cm above the line.
Construct a line perpendicular to XY that passes through P.

6 Draw an angle of 80°. Construct its bisector.

7 Draw an angle of 140°. Construct its bisector.

8 Draw an angle of 200°. Construct its bisector.

9 Mark a point A. Draw the locus of points that are 3 cm from the point A.

10 Draw a horizontal line AB 4 cm long. Draw the locus of points that are 2 cm from the line AB.

11 Mark a point Q. Show by shading the locus of points that are less than 3.5 cm from the point Q.

12 Draw a rectangle ABCD where AB = 6 cm and BC = 3 cm. Shade the locus of points inside the rectangle that are more than 2 cm from A.

13 a Construct triangle ABC.
  b Shade the region inside the triangle that is more than 4 cm from A and closer to BC than AC.

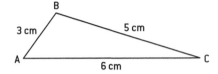

14 a Draw accurately a square WXYZ with sides 5 cm.
  b Shade the locus of points inside the square that are less than 4cm from W and closer to WX than WZ.

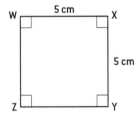

15 The diagram shows a goat tied to a rectangular shed by a rope. The rope which is attached to the shed at point C is 7 m long. Draw the shed using a scale of 1 cm = 1 m. The shed is located in the middle of a large field. Shade the area where the goat can graze.

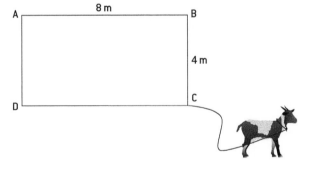

Ratio and proportion 2

1 Share each of the amounts in the given ratio.
   a £20 in the ratio 1:4   b £18 in the ratio 5:1
   c £28 in the ratio 2:5   d £90 in the ratio 3:7
   e £120 in the ratio 7:5   f £3000 in the ratio 4:11
   g £42 in the ratio 1:2:4   h £240 in the ratio 2:3:7

2 Tessa and Vivienne share £96 in the ratio 5:3. How much more does Tessa receive than Vivienne?

3 The three angles in a triangle are in the ratio 1:3:6. What is the size of the largest angle in the triangle?

4 Jane, Kim and Louise share 36 sweets in the ratio 4:2:3. How many sweets does Louise receive?

5 The four angles in a quadrilateral are in the ratio 1:2:2:3. Work out the size of the four angles.

6 Three apples cost 81p. What is the cost of two apples?

7 Five pens cost £3.25. What is the cost of nine pens?

8 Noel can run 5 km in 30 minutes. Running at the same speed, how long will it take him to run 8 km?

9 A bale wrapper takes 12 minutes to wrap 4 round bales. How long will it take to wrap 7 bales?

10 The following ingredients are needed to make 12 pancakes.
                225 g plain flour
                3 eggs
                30 g sugar
                360 ml buttermilk
   Work out the amount of each ingredient needed to make 20 pancakes.

11 The following ingredients are needed to make a lasagne for 4 people.
                400 g minced steak
                300 g tomatoes
                1 onion
                600 ml cheese sauce
   Work out the amount of each ingredient needed to make a lasagne for 10 people.

12 In each of the following, which is better value for money? You must show your working.
   a 6 oranges costing £2.40 **or** 8 oranges costing £3.04
   b 2 litres of milk for £1.16 **or** 3 litres of milk for £1.70
   c 50 minutes for £1.40 **or** 60 minutes for £1.56
   d 500 g of butter for £2.20 **or** 200 g of butter for 96p

CHAPTER 50 | Inequalities

This chapter is about

- reading and writing inequalities
- showing inequalities on a number line
- solving inequalities.

Exercise A

1 Write an inequality for each statement.
   - **a** x is less than 4
   - **b** y is greater than 2
   - **c** m is less than or equal to 8
   - **d** t is more than -5
   - **e** w is less than -6
   - **f** c is greater than or equal to 10

2 Write down the **integers** which satisfy the following.
   - **a** $1 \leqslant x \leqslant 4$
   - **b** $0 \leqslant x \leqslant 3$
   - **c** $2 < x < 5$
   - **d** $1 < x \leqslant 3$
   - **e** $3 \leqslant x < 7$
   - **f** $-2 \leqslant x \leqslant 1$
   - **g** $-5 \leqslant x < 0$
   - **h** $-8 < x \leqslant -6$
   - **i** $-4 < x < -1$
   - **j** $-5 \leqslant x < -4$
   - **k** $3 < x \leqslant 5$
   - **l** $4 < x < 6$

3 Write down the **integers** which satisfy the following.
   - **a** $0 < x < 2\frac{1}{2}$
   - **b** $1\frac{1}{4} < x < 5\frac{1}{4}$
   - **c** $-3\frac{1}{2} \leqslant x \leqslant -1$
   - **d** $-6\frac{1}{5} < x \leqslant -2\frac{1}{4}$
   - **e** $\frac{7}{2} \leqslant x \leqslant \frac{11}{2}$
   - **f** $\frac{5}{3} < x < \frac{20}{3}$
   - **g** $-\frac{11}{4} < x \leqslant \frac{7}{6}$
   - **h** $-\frac{20}{7} \leqslant x \leqslant -\frac{6}{5}$
   - **i** $-4\frac{1}{4} \leqslant x < 2\frac{2}{5}$

4 Solve each inequality.
   - **a** $x + 5 > 5$
   - **b** $x - 2 \geqslant 8$
   - **c** $x + 4 < 4$
   - **d** $x - 6 > 4$
   - **e** $x + 5 \leqslant 1$
   - **f** $x - 1 \geqslant -6$
   - **g** $2x > 10$
   - **h** $3x < 12$
   - **i** $6x \geqslant 24$
   - **j** $\frac{x}{3} > 6$
   - **k** $\frac{x}{2} \leqslant 8$
   - **l** $\frac{x}{4} \geqslant -10$
   - **m** $2x + 1 > 9$
   - **n** $3x - 2 \leqslant 13$
   - **o** $5x - 4 \geqslant 21$
   - **p** $6x - 8 < 8$
   - **q** $3x + 4 > 12$
   - **r** $5x - 5 \leqslant 1$
   - **s** $2x - 7 > 10$
   - **t** $2(x + 3) \geqslant 14$
   - **u** $3(x - 2) < 15$
   - **v** $5x + 1 \leqslant 2x + 13$
   - **w** $2x - 7 > x - 4$
   - **x** $6 + 3x < 10 - x$
   - **y** $2(3x - 1) > 4(x + 4)$
   - **z** $5(3 + 2x) \leqslant 2(3 - x)$

5 Solve each inequality.
   - **a** $4 < 2x < 12$
   - **b** $6 \leqslant 3x \leqslant 24$
   - **c** $5 < 5x \leqslant 15$
   - **d** $6 < 2x < 11$
   - **e** $-1 < 4x \leqslant 8$
   - **f** $2 < 3x < 10$
   - **g** $7 \leqslant 5x < 20$
   - **h** $5 \leqslant 6x \leqslant 12$
   - **i** $-3 \leqslant 4x < 0$

Exercise B

1 Write down the inequality that is represented by each of the number lines.

a

b

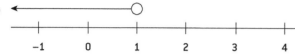

c

d

e

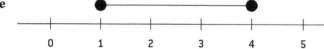

f

g

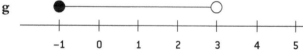

h

2 Show each inequality on a number line.
   a $x \leqslant 2$ **b** $x > -1$ **c** $1 < x \leqslant 3$
   d $-4 < x < -1$ **e** $-3 \leqslant x < 0$ **f** $-2\frac{1}{2} < x < 1\frac{1}{2}$

3 Solve each inequality and show the solution on a number line.
   a $2x + 3 \geqslant 11$ **b** $3x - 2 < 1$
   c $-4 \leqslant 2x < 8$ **d** $-9 < 3x \leqslant 6$
   e $5x - 1 \leqslant 3x + 7$ **f** $3(2x - 1) > 5(x - 1)$

4 Given that x is an **integer** solve each inequality and show the solution on a number line.
   a $-2 < 2x < 10$ **b** $-6 \leqslant 3x < 0$
   c $1 < 2x < 7$ **d** $0 \leqslant 5x < 13$
   e $4 < 3x \leqslant 15$ **f** $15 \leqslant 7x < 30$

CHAPTER 51

Real-life graphs

This chapter is about

■ drawing and using real-life graphs including conversion graphs and distance-time graphs.

1 A duck egg costs 30p.

a Copy and complete the table showing the cost of different numbers of duck eggs.

Number of duck eggs	1	2	3	4	5
Cost (pence)	30				

b Use the information in the table to draw a straight-line graph.

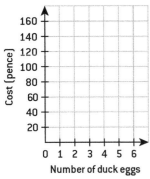

c Use your graph to find the cost of 18 duck eggs.

2 A car hire company charges a fixed rate of £50 and then £25 for every day a car is hired.

a Copy and complete the table showing the cost of hiring a car for different numbers of days.

Number of days	1	2	3	4	5
Cost (£)					

b Use the information in the table to draw a straight-line graph.

3 The exchange rate between pounds and Thai baht is £1 = 40THB.

Pounds (£)	1	2	3	4	5
Thai baht (THB)	40				

a Copy and complete the table.

b Use the information in the table to draw a conversion graph.

c Use your graph to convert

   i 100 THB into £

   ii £11 into THB

   iii £70 into THB.

4 The conversion table below shows speeds in mph and km/h.

Miles per hour	25	50	75	100	125
Kilometres per hour	40	80	120	160	200

   a Use the information in the table to draw a conversion graph.
   b Use your graph to convert 60 mph into km/h.
   c Use your graph to convert 140 km/h into mph.
   d The current land speed record is approximately 1200 km/h. Use your graph to convert this speed to mph.
   e In South Korea a high-speed train called the HEMU–420X reached a speed of 250 mph. Use your graph to convert this speed to km/h.

5 a Copy and complete the conversion table for metres and feet.

Metres	3	6	9	12	15
Feet	10				

   b Use the information in the table to draw a conversion graph.
   c Use your graph to convert 5 metres into feet.
   d Use your graph to convert 42 feet into metres.
   e Use your graph to convert 200 metres into feet.

6 Study the two conversion graphs.

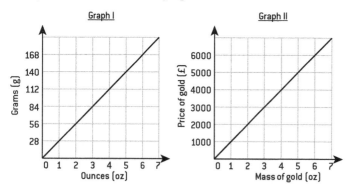

   a Use graph I to convert 30 oz into grams.
   b Use graph II to work out the value of 25 oz of gold.
   c Lord Bullion has 14 kg of gold in a secure bank. Use graphs I and II to work out the value of his stock.

7 Look at this distance–time graph. The graph shows the journey of a car from home.

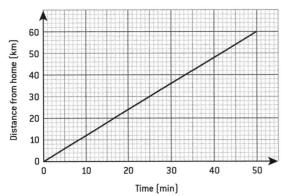

a How far had the car travelled after 22 minutes?
b How long did it take the car to travel 20 km?
c Calculate the average speed of the car for the journey.

8 Look at this distance–time graph. It shows Teresa's journey home from work.

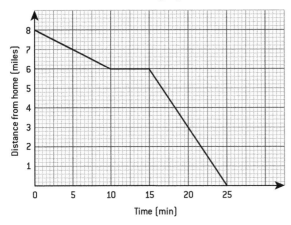

a How far from work does Teresa live?
b On the way home she stopped for petrol. How long did she stop?
c How far had she travelled from work when she stopped for petrol?
d Calculate the average speed of the last part of the journey from the filling station to home.

9 This distance–time graph shows Gerard's journey on Saturday morning.

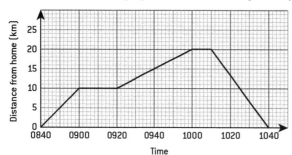

a What time did Gerard leave home?

b He dropped his son off at the leisure centre for football practice at 9.00 a.m. and then drove to his friend's house to pick up a part for his computer.

  i How long did he stop at the leisure centre?

  ii How long did it take him to drive to his friend's house after he left the leisure centre?

  iii How far does his friend live from the leisure centre?

c Between which two times was the quickest part of the journey?

d Calculate Gerard's average speed from the leisure centre to his friend's house.

10 This distance–time graph shows Neil's journey to town and back by bus.

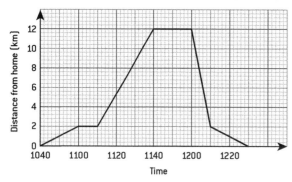

a Neil leaves home at 1040 and walks to the bus stop. He catches the number 23 bus into the town centre. He pays his electricity bill while he is in the town centre. He then takes the bus back home.

  i How far is it from the bus stop to the town centre?

  ii How long does Neil spend in the town?

  iii How long does it take Neil to get home from the town?

  iv Calculate the average speed of the bus on the journey back from the town.

b Neil's mother leaves home at 0840 and takes his sister to school. The school is 8 km from home. She arrives at school at 0855. She then leaves the school at 0905 and returns home at an average speed of 24 km/h.

Illustrate this journey on a distance–time graph.

CHAPTER 52 Probability

This chapter is about

- using a probability scale
- using terms such as random, fair, biased
- knowing the probability of an event which is impossible
- knowing the probability of an event which is certain
- finding the probability of an event happening
- knowing what is meant by mutually exclusive outcomes
- knowing that the probability of something happening is 1 minus the probability of it not happening
- knowing that the sum of all the probabilities of an event is 1
- drawing a probability space diagram
- finding the expected frequency of an event
- using relative frequency as an estimate of probability.

Exercise A

1   Look at the following words:

likely   certain   impossible   evens   unlikely

Copy the scale and write each word in the appropriate position on the line:

0	0.5	1

2 | impossible   certain   likely   unlikely   evens |

Choose the most suitable word from the list to describe the probability of
a   Someone being born on 30 February.
b   Wednesday coming after Tuesday.
c   Randomly taking an even number from the numbers between 1 and 10.
d   It raining in Belfast in February.
e   Getting a six when rolling a fair dice.

3   A bag contains 3 red, 2 green and 4 blue pens. A pen is taken at random from the bag. What is the probability that it is
a   green   **b**   red   **c**   yellow   **d**   blue or green?

4   An ordinary fair dice is rolled. What is the probability of rolling
a   a five   **b**   an odd number   **c**   a multiple of 4   **d**   a number less than 3?

5   In a class there are 10 girls and 12 boys. A pupil is chosen at random from the class. What is the probability that the pupil is a girl?

6   A letter is taken at random from the word PARALLELOGRAM. What is the probability that it is
a   the letter R   **b**   the letter L   **c**   the letter S   **d**   a vowel?

7 A pentagonal spinner is divided into 5 equal-sized sections. Three of the sections are coloured black and two are coloured red. It is spun once. What it the probability of it landing on
  a black   **b** red   **c** yellow?

8 A child has a box containing lego bricks which are all the same size. There are 7 yellow bricks, 5 blue bricks and 8 red bricks. The child takes out a brick at random. Calculate the probability that he takes out
  a a yellow brick   **b** a blue brick
  c a yellow or red brick   **d** a green brick.

9 An ordinary fair dice is rolled once. Find the probability of getting
  a the number 5   **b** a prime number   **c** a square number
  d a number greater than 4   **e** 4 or less.

10 In a classroom there are 26 pupils. There are 14 girls and 12 boys. Each pupil is given a different number between 1 and 26. A number is randomly taken from a hat. Calculate the probability that
  a the number is 12   **b** the number is even
  c the number belongs to a boy   **d** the number is more than 10.

11 A farmer has 200 dairy cows. Each cow is given a different tag number between 1 and 200. A cow is taken at random from the herd. Calculate the probability that the cow
  a has a tag with an even number   **b** has a tag number more than 170
  c has a tag number less than 80   **d** is female.

12 Brian and Melissa play a game of tennis. Brian says that the probability of him winning is a half. Is he correct? Explain your answer.

13 In a game of football a team can only win, lose or draw a match. Explain however, why the probability of a team winning a game is not equal to $\frac{1}{3}$.

Exercise B

1 Copy and complete the table below.

	Probability that event A happens	Probability that event A does not happen
a	70%	
b	12%	
c	$\frac{7}{9}$	
d	$\frac{11}{15}$	
e	0.65	
f	0.8	
g	0.04	
h		$\frac{11}{30}$
i		37%

2 The probability of the number 23 bus being late on any given day is 0.3. Calculate the probability that the number 23 bus will not be late.

3 The probability that George wins a game of chess against his dad is 0.42. Calculate the probability George will not win the game.

4 The probability of getting heads on a biased coin is 64%. Find the probability of getting tails on the same coin.

5 The probability that a teacher will give homework on a Tuesday night during term time is 0.85.

Calculate the probability that the same teacher will not give homework on a Tuesday night during term time.

6 The table below shows the probabilities of getting different colours when one sweet is taken at random from a large bag of sweets.

Colour of sweet	Red	Yellow	Green	Orange
Probability	0.3	0.35		0.2

a Calculate the probability of getting a green sweet.
b Calculate the probability of not getting a red sweet.

7 Karen rolls a fair dice and tosses a coin at the same time.

		Dice					
		1	2	3	4	5	6
Coin	Head						
	Tail						

a Complete the sample space diagram to show all the possible outcomes.
b Calculate the probability that Karen
   i gets heads with an even number
   ii gets tails and a 3.

8 A fair five-sided spinner is numbered 2, 2, 3, 3, 3. An ordinary fair dice is numbered 1 to 6. The spinner is spun and the dice is rolled. The two scores are added together.
a Draw a sample space diagram to show all the possible totals.
b Using your sample space diagram calculate the probability of getting a total
   i of six
   ii that is even
   iii less than 3.

9 A bag contains 2 red, 2 blue and 2 yellow sweets. A second bag contains 3 yellow and 2 blue sweets. One sweet is taken at random from the first bag and then one sweet is taken at random from the second bag.

		Second bag				
		Y	Y	Y	B	B
First bag	R					
	R					
	B					
	B					
	Y					
	Y					

  a Complete the sample space diagram to show all the possible outcomes.
  b Using your sample space diagram calculate the probability of getting
    i a red and a blue sweet
    ii at least one yellow sweet
    iii two sweets the same colour
    iv no blue sweets.

10 An ordinary fair dice numbered 1 to 6 is rolled and a regular three-sided spinner labelled A, B and C is spun.
  a Draw a sample space diagram to show all the possible outcomes.
  b From your sample space diagram calculate the probability of getting
    i number 4 and the letter A
    ii an even number and the letter C
    iii a number more than 2 and A or B
    iv a prime number and a vowel.

Exercise C

1 The table below shows the probabilities of taking different coloured counters from a bag of counters.

Colour of counter	Red	Blue	Black	White
Probability	$\dfrac{3}{20}$	$\dfrac{7}{20}$		$\dfrac{1}{20}$

  a Calculate the probability of taking a black counter from the bag.
  b Given that the bag contains 120 counters, calculate how many blue counters are in the bag.

2 The table below shows how pupils travel to St Louis High School each morning and the probability of each method.

Method of transport	Walk	Bicycle	Bus	Car
Probability	0.12	0.2	0.55	

  a Calculate the probability that a pupil will travel to school by car.
  b Given that there are 800 pupils at St Louis High School, how many pupils would you expect to travel to school by bicycle?

3 The table below shows the percentages of animals a farmer owns.

Type of animal	Sheep	Pig	Cow	Horse
Percentage	24%		38%	2%

   a Calculate the probability that an animal taken at random from the farm is a pig.
   b Given that the farmer has 250 animals in total, how many sheep does he have?

4 At a vending machine four types of soft drink are sold. The probability that each type of drink is sold is given below.

Type of drink	Cola	Lemonade	Energy+	Orange Burst
Probability	0.12	0.3	0.2	

   a Calculate the missing probability for Orange Burst.
   b 150 drinks were sold on a given day. How many cans of cola would you expect to have been sold?

5 In a large comprehensive school there are 900 pupils. The probability that a pupil is male is 0.45. The probability that a pupil has blue eyes is 0.4. Calculate
   a the number of girls in the school
   b the number of pupils in the school with blue eyes
   c the number of boys in the school with blue eyes.

6 In a factory which employs 400 staff the probability of an employee working on the assembly line is 0.8. The probability that an employee is male is 0.65. Calculate
   a the number of employees who work on the assembly line
   b the number of female employees working at the factory
   c the number of male employees who do not work on the assembly line.

7 Hannah rolls a dice 30 times. The results are recorded below.

Number on dice	1	2	3	4	5	6
Frequency	2	7	3	5	1	12

   a Work out the relative frequency of
     i getting a 2   **ii** getting a 6   **iii** getting an even number.
   b **i** Is the dice biased? Give a reason for your answer.
     ii How can Hannah improve her experiment to get a more accurate relative frequency?

8 Colum is doing an experiment. He wants to know when he drops his boot if it will land on its side or land upright. The table shows his results.

Number of trials	Landed upright	Landed on side
10	5	5
50	30	20
100	62	38
200	125	75

   a Calculate the relative frequency of the boot landing upright after 10, 50, 100 and 200 trials.
   b Colum says that the relative frequency of his boot landing upright is 0.5.
     Is he correct? Give a reason for your answer.

CHAPTER 53 — Effect of enlargement on similar shapes

This chapter is about

■ knowing the effect of enlargement on perimeter, area and volume
■ using ratios to calculate the perimeter, area and volume of similar 2D shapes and 3D shapes.

1 Rectangles A and B are similar.

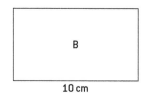

5 cm   10 cm

a Given that the perimeter of A is 14 cm, find the perimeter of B.

b Given that the area of A is 10 cm², find the area of B.

2 P and Q are similar triangles.

The length of the base of Q is 3 times longer than the length of the base of P.

Given that the area of P is 11 cm², work out the area of Q.

3 M and N are similar parallelograms.

The base of N is 5 times longer than the base of M. Given that the perimeter of M is 50 cm work out the perimeter of N.

4 T and R are regular hexagons.

T is enlarged by a scale factor of 4 to give R. The area of T is 10 cm². What is the area of R?

5 G and H are similar rectangles.

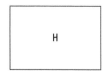

The ratio of the breadth of G to the breadth of H is 1:6. Given that the perimeter of H is 72 cm, what is the perimeter of G?

6 A rectangle has area 12 cm². It is enlarged by a scale factor of 3. Calculate the area of the enlarged rectangle.

7 Triangles K and L are similar.

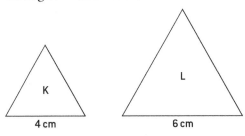

4 cm 6 cm

The area of K is 20 cm². What is the area of L?

8 Cones A and B are similar.

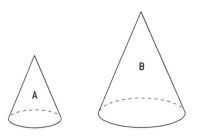

The height of B is 3 times the height of A.
a The surface area of A is 10 cm². Find the surface area of B.
b The volume of A is 2 cm³. Find the volume of B.

9 Cuboids C and D are similar.

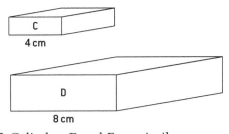

4 cm

8 cm

The volume of C is 80 cm³. Calculate the volume of D.

10 Cylinders E and F are similar.

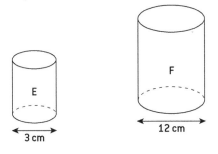

3 cm 12 cm

The surface area of E is 150 cm². Calculate the surface area of F.

11 Solids U and V are similar and are both made of plastic.

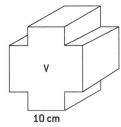

2 cm 10 cm

a Given that U weighs 120 g, calculate the mass of V.

b Given that U has a surface area of 80 cm², calculate the surface area of V.

CHAPTER 54 Quadratic graphs

This chapter is about

- drawing and using quadratic graphs.

1 Which of the following are quadratic equations?

$y = x^2 + 5$ $y = 3x - 1$ $y = 3x - x^2$

$y = \dfrac{3}{x}$ $y = x^3 - 2$ $y = x^2 + 6x + 3$

2 Copy and complete the table of values for each of the quadratic equations below.

x	−3	−2	−1	0	1	2	3
y							

a $y = x^2$ **b** $y = x^2 + 4$ **c** $y = x^2 + x$
d $y = x^2 + 3x$ **e** $y = x^2 + 2x + 1$ **f** $y = x^2 - 2x$
g $y = x^2 + x - 5$ **h** $y = 10 - x^2$ **i** $y = 2x - x^2$

3 **a** Copy and complete the table of values for $y = x^2 + 3$

x	−3	−2	−1	0	1	2
y						

  b Draw the graph on a set of axes with x-axis from −3 to 3 and y-axis from 0 to 12
  c Use the graph to find the value of y when $x = 2.5$
  d Use the graph to find the values of x when $y = 8$

4 **a** Copy and complete the table of values for $y = x^2 + 2x - 5$

x	−4	−3	−2	−1	0	1	2	3
y								

  b Draw the graph on a set of axes with x-axis from −4 to 3 and y-axis from −6 to 12
  c Use the graph to solve $x^2 + 2x - 5 = 0$
  d Use the graph to find the value of y when $x = 0.5$
  e Use the graph to find the values of x when $y = -1$

5 **a** Copy and complete the table of values for $y = x^2 - 3x - 4$

x	−2	−1	0	1	2	3	4	5
y								

  b Draw the graph on a set of axes with x-axis from −2 to 5 and y-axis from −7 to 7
  c Use the graph to solve $x^2 - 3x - 4 = 0$
  d Use the graph to find the value of y when $x = 1.5$
  e Use the graph to find the values of x when $y = 3$

CHAPTER 55 Perimeter, area and volume 2

This chapter is about

■ finding the perimeter and area of compound shapes
■ knowing and using the formulae for the area of a parallelogram, rhombus, kite and trapezium
■ calculating the surface area and volume of solid shapes.

Exercise A

1 Find the area of each shape.

a
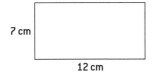
7 cm

12 cm

b
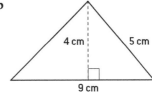
4 cm   5 cm

9 cm

2 Find the area of each shape.

a
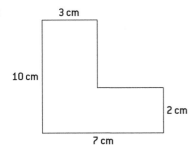
3 cm

10 cm

2 cm

7 cm

b
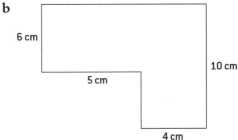
6 cm

10 cm

5 cm

4 cm

c
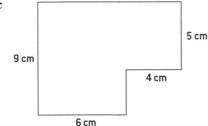
5 cm

9 cm

4 cm

6 cm

d
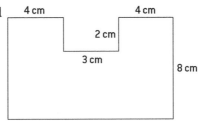
4 cm   4 cm

2 cm

3 cm

8 cm

e

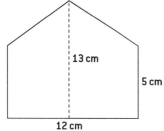

13 cm

5 cm

12 cm

f

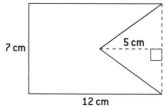

7 cm

5 cm

12 cm

3 Find the area of each shaded shape.

a

10 cm

2 cm

6 cm

4 cm

b

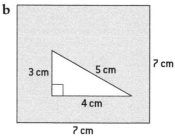

3 cm

5 cm

7 cm

4 cm

7 cm

4 Find the perimeter of each shape.

a

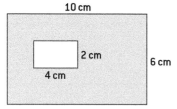

4.5 cm

13 cm

b

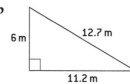

6 m

12.7 m

11.2 m

5 Find the perimeter and the area of each shape.

a

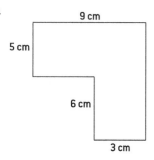

9 cm

5 cm

6 cm

3 cm

b

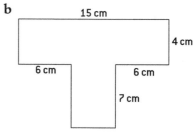

15 cm

4 cm

6 cm

6 cm

7 cm

c

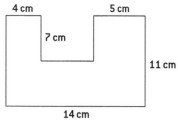

4 cm

5 cm

7 cm

11 cm

14 cm

d

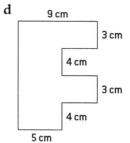

9 cm

3 cm

4 cm

3 cm

4 cm

5 cm

Exercise B

1 Find the area of each shape.

a
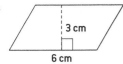
3 cm
6 cm

b
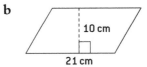
10 cm
21 cm

c
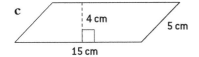
4 cm
5 cm
15 cm

d
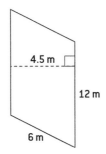
4.5 m
12 m
6 m

e
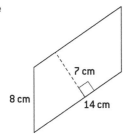
7 cm
8 cm
14 cm

f
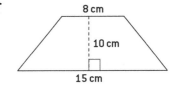
8 cm
10 cm
15 cm

g
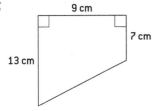
9 cm
7 cm
13 cm

h
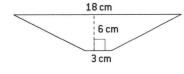
18 cm
6 cm
3 cm

i
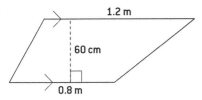
1.2 m
60 cm
0.8 m

j
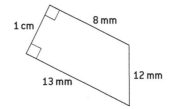
1 cm
8 mm
13 mm
12 mm

2 Find the area of each shape.

a

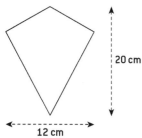

20 cm

12 cm

b

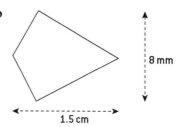

8 mm

1.5 cm

c

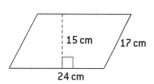

8 cm

15 cm

32 cm

d

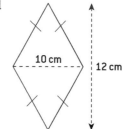

10 cm

12 cm

3 Find: **i** the perimeter
        ii the area of each shape.

a

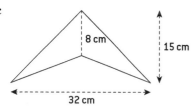

15 cm   17 cm

24 cm

b

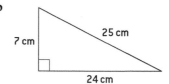

7 cm   25 cm

24 cm

c

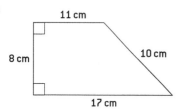

11 cm

8 cm   10 cm

17 cm

d

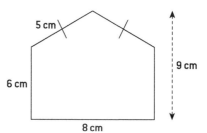

5 cm

6 cm   9 cm

8 cm

4 Find *h* in each of the following.

a

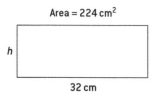

Area = 224 cm²

h

32 cm

b

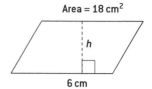

Area = 18 cm²

h

6 cm

c

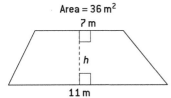

Area = 36 m²

7 m

h

11 m

d

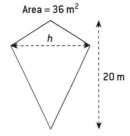

Area = 36 m²

h

20 m

5 Calculate the shaded area in this stencil.

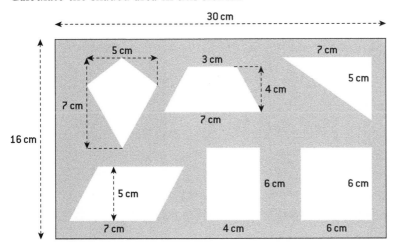

30 cm

5 cm

3 cm

7 cm

5 cm

4 cm

7 cm

7 cm

16 cm

5 cm

6 cm

6 cm

7 cm

4 cm

6 cm

Exercise C

1 Work out the total surface area of each of the following. State the units.

a

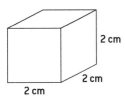

2 cm

2 cm

2 cm

b

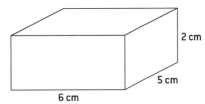

2 cm

5 cm

6 cm

c

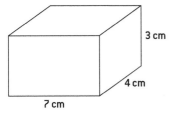

3 cm

4 cm

7 cm

d

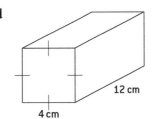

12 cm

4 cm

2 Find the surface area of each of the following.
  a a cube of side 4 cm
  b a cuboid measuring 9 cm by 4 cm by 2 cm
  c a cuboid measuring 7.5 cm by 2 cm by 2 cm
  d a cuboid measuring 60 cm by 70 cm by 1.2 m

3 Find the surface area of each of these triangular prisms.

a

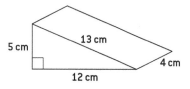

b

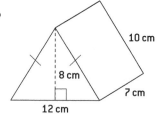

4 Find the volume of each prism.

a

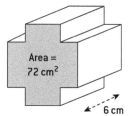

b

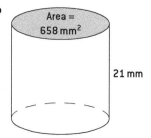

5 Calculate the volume of a prism that has cross-sectional area 125 cm² and length 9 cm.

6 Calculate the volume of a prism that has cross-sectional area 340 mm² and length 1.4 cm.

7 Calculate the volume of each of the following.

a

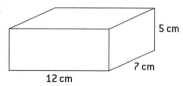

b

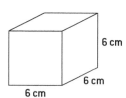

c

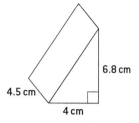

d

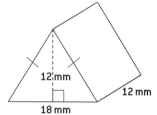

8 Calculate the volume of each prism.

a

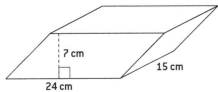

b

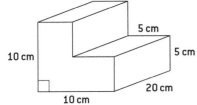

9 Find the volume of each trapezoidal prism.

a

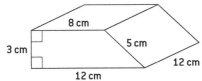

b

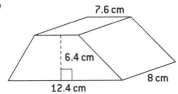

10 A prism has volume 2400 cm³ and cross-sectional area 192 cm². Calculate its length.

11 A prism has volume 780 mm³ and length 32.5 mm. Calculate its cross-sectional area.

CHAPTER 56

Time, distance, speed and density

This chapter is about

- knowing the formulae connecting distance, speed and time
- using the formulae to find distance, speed and time
- knowing the formulae connecting mass, density and volume
- using the formulae to find mass, density and volume.

Exercise A

1 Work out the time in minutes for each of the following.

    a 2 hours   **b** $3\frac{1}{2}$ hours   **c** $\frac{1}{4}$ hour   **d** $\frac{3}{5}$ hour

    e 1.2 hours   **f** 1.6 hours   **g** 2.8 hours   **h** 0.3 hours

2 What fraction of an hour is each of the following times? Give each fraction in its simplest form.

    a 15 minutes   **b** 10 minutes   **c** 24 minutes   **d** 55 minutes
    e 3 minutes   **f** 1 minute   **g** 18 minutes   **h** 30 seconds

3 Find the average speed in mph for each journey.

    a 80 miles in 2 hours   **b** 150 miles in 5 hours
    c 23 miles in 30 minutes   **d** 14 miles in 15 minutes

    e 90 miles in $1\frac{1}{2}$ hours   **f** 160 miles in $2\frac{1}{2}$ hours

    g 17 miles in 20 minutes   **h** 90 miles in $1\frac{1}{4}$ hours

4 Find the average speed in km/h for each journey.

    a 150 km in 3 hours   **b** 152 km in 4 hours
    c 11 km in 10 minutes   **d** 13 km in 12 minutes

    e 75 km in 2 hours   **f** 72 km in $\frac{3}{4}$ hour

    g 210 km in $3\frac{1}{2}$ hours   **h** 7 km in 5 minutes

5 Faith travels 15 miles in 20 minutes. Calculate her average speed in mph.

6 Andrew is on a high speed train. It travels 280 miles in $2\frac{1}{2}$ hours. Calculate the average speed of the train.

7 Find the time taken to travel 100 miles at an average speed of 60 mph.

8 Find the distance travelled on a journey that took $1\frac{1}{2}$ hours at an average speed of 70 km/h.

9 Barney travels 15 km in 18 minutes. Calculate his average speed in km/h.

10 Copy and complete the following table that shows the average speed, time taken and length of each journey.

	Average speed	Time taken	Length of journey
a	55 mph	30 min	
b	50 mph	$1\frac{1}{4}$ hours	
c	60 km/h		150 km
d	70 km/h		87.5 km
e		45 min	60 km
f		20 min	18 miles
g	18 km/h	10 min	
h	84 km/h		21 km

Exercise B

1 Find the density in g/cm³ of a substance which has mass 600 g and volume 120 cm³.

2 Find the density of a substance with mass 3 kg and volume 100 cm³
   a in kg/cm³ **b** in g/cm³.

3 A block of density 2.4 g/cm³ has volume 500 cm³. Find its mass in grams.

4 A block of density 6.5 g/cm³ has volume 320 cm³. Find its mass
   a in grams **b** in kilograms.

5 A mass of 280 g has density 3.5 g/cm³. Find its volume.

6 A mass of 3 kg has density 7.5 g/cm³. Find its volume.

7 Find the density of each object in g/cm³.

a

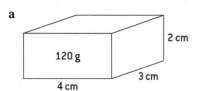

2 cm
120 g
3 cm
4 cm

b

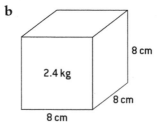

8 cm
2.4 kg
8 cm
8 cm

c

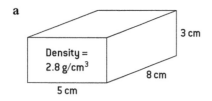

15 cm
1470 g
7 cm
4 cm

d

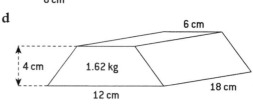

6 cm
4 cm
1.62 kg
18 cm
12 cm

8 A cuboid measures 8 cm by 6 cm by 2 cm. Its mass is 75 g. Find its density in g/cm³.

9 A cube has sides of length 5 cm. Its mass is 75 g. Find its density in g/cm³.

10 Find the mass of each object.

a

3 cm
Density =
2.8 g/cm³
8 cm
5 cm

b

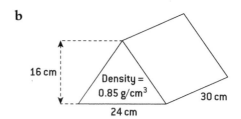

16 cm
Density =
0.85 g/cm³
30 cm
24 cm

11 A cuboid's length is 10 cm and its breadth is 6 cm. The density of the cuboid is 2.5 g/cm³. Given that the cuboid's mass is 900 g, find its height.